Essential

G000161731

Above: *Midtown Manhattan from across the East River*

AAA Publishing
1000 AAA Drive, Heathrow, Florida 32746

This edition first published in 2001 by AAA Publishing,
1000 AAA Drive, Heathrow, FL 32746-5063 U.S.A.

Front cover: *Coney Island;
Times Square; Grand
Central Station; Statue of
Liberty*

Back cover: *yellow taxis*

The contents of this publication are believed correct at
the time of printing. Nevertheless, the publishers cannot
accept responsibility for errors or omissions, nor for
changes in details given. We are always grateful to
readers who let us know of any errors or omissions
they come across, and future printings will be updated
accordingly.

Published by AAA Publishing in conjunction with
The Automobile Association of Great Britain.

Written by Mick Sinclair

Library of Congress Catalog Card Number: on file
ISBN 1–56251–876–3

Color separation: BTB Digital Imaging, Whitchurch,
Hampshire

Printed and bound in Italy by Printer Trento S.r.l.

A01088

Find out more about
AAA Publishing and the
wide range of services
AAA provides by visiting
our website at
www.AAA.com

The weather chart on **page 118** of this book is
calibrated in °C. For conversion to °F simply use the
following formula:

$$°F = 1.8 \times °C + 32$$

Contents

About this Book

Essential *New York* is divided into five sections to cover the most important aspects of your visit to New York.

Viewing New York pages 5–14

An introduction to New York by the author
New York's Features
Essence of New York
The Shaping of New York
Peace and Quiet
New York's Famous

Top Ten pages 15–26

The author's choice of the Top Ten places to see in New York, listed in alphabetical order, each with practical information.

What to See pages 27–90

The five main areas of New York, each with its own brief introduction and an alphabetical listing of the main attractions
Practical information
Snippets of 'Did You Know...' information
7 suggested walks
2 features

Where To... pages 91–116

Detailed listings of the best places to eat, stay, shop, take the children and be entertained.

Practical Matters pages 117–24

A highly visual section containing essential travel information.

Maps

All map references are to the individual maps found in the What to See section of this guide.

For example, Central Park has the reference ➕ 70B4 – indicating the page on which the map is located and the grid square in which the park is to be found. A list of the maps that have been used in this travel guide can be found in the index.

Prices

Where appropriate, an indication of the cost of an establishment is given by **£** signs:

£££ denotes higher prices, **££** denotes average prices, while **£** denotes lower charges.

Star Ratings

Most of the places described in this book have been given a separate rating:

❂❂❂   Do not miss

❂❂   Highly recommended

❂   Worth seeing

Viewing
New York

Above: *Central Park*
Right: *shoe-shine on Broadway*

Mick Sinclair's New York

Safe New York?
Once notoriously crime-infested, New York now seems to be undergoing a remarkable change. Crime rates have fallen drastically and, in 1996, murders in the city fell below 1,000 for the first time in 30 years. Observers cite a combination of a crackdown on petty crime and a restructuring of police precinct administration as reasons for the transformation, although the improvement also reflects a nationwide drop in crime.

Probably no city in the world is as economically powerful, as ethnically diverse, as sung about, talked about, written about, photographed, filmed, eulogised, mythologised, loved and loathed – or simply as famous – as New York.

This city is a magnet not only for tourists seduced by images of Times Square and the Chrysler Building, or making a pilgrimage to the site of the World Trade Center, but for anyone in search of a better life. Small-town Americans arrive seeking the professional opportunities only New York holds, or for the chance to pursue unconventional lifestyles without fear of ridicule.

For those from further afield, New York can mean improved possibilities for themselves and for future generations of their families. Since its earliest days, waves of immigration have shaped New York into a multi-ethnic city. The hundreds of thousands of Europeans that came in the late 1800s have been followed in more recent decades by Puerto Ricans, Chinese, Indians, and countless others, greatly broadening the city's ethnic make-up.

As well as transforming lives, New York regularly transforms itself. The 1980s and 1990s saw an office-building boom while more localised development saw the regeneration of SoHo, TriBeCa, Chelsea and Times Square. Meanwhile, the Financial District recovers steadily from the devastation of 11 September 2001.

The best thing a New York visitor can do is just join in. Ride the subways and the buses, explore the nooks and crannies of offbeat neighbourhoods, and discover why nobody can ever accuse New York of being boring.

The annual St Patrick's Day Parade: New York City fire-fighters honour their colleagues who died on 11 September 2001

New York's Features

Geography
Area of New York City:
321 square miles
Area of Manhattan: 22.7
square miles
Miles of street: 6,400
Miles of waterfront: 578

Public Transport
Number of subway
stations: 490
Miles of subway track: 685
Number of subway cars:
5,871
Buses: 4,871
Weekday passengers: 7.3
million
Miles of bus routes: 1,671

Population
The Bronx: 1.33 million
Brooklyn: 2.5 million
Manhattan: 1.5 million
Queens: 2.2 million
Staten Island: 444,000

Ethnicity
Caucasian: 2.8 million
African–American:
2.1 million
Hispanic: 2.2 million
Asian: 800,000
Other: 900,000

New York Taxis
The New York Taxi and
Limousine Commission (TLC)
is responsible for regulating
the city's 12,187 yellow cabs,
around 40,000 other vehicles
licensed to carry paying
passengers, and some
100,000 drivers. Yellow cabs
are inspected for safety and
emissions three times a year
by the TLC, which also seizes
400–600 vehicles a month for
operating illegally.

Buildings
Commercial: 31,000 Industrial: 22,000
Public facilities and institutions: 11,000
Residential: 710,000

New York at Work
With private companies: over 3 million
City, state and federal bodies: 600,000
Self-employed: 400,000

Broadway Theatre Audiences
Average age: 40 Female: 61 per cent
From New York: 31 per cent College degree: 36 per cent
Average household income: $94,000

Top: *yellow cabs wait for*
the lights to change on a
rainy day in Midtown
Manhattan
Above: *the busy streets*
of Chinatown

Essence of New York

Many visitors arrive in New York already knowing exactly what they want to do and see. Climbing skyscrapers, going to Broadway shows, shopping, touring world-class museums and staying in luxury hotels can all be accomplished in New York with perhaps more style and glamour than in any other city. Yet New York is a city of infinite guises, where contrasting side-by-side neighbourhoods house people from seemingly every nation on earth and where local markets, secret parks, one-room museums and unsung architectural marvels await discovery at every turn once the obvious destinations have been exhausted.

THE **10** ESSENTIALS

If you only have a short time to visit New York, and would like to get a quick picture of the city, here are the essentials:

Left: *Central Park rollerbladers relax*

Below: *taking a break in Bleecker Street in Greenwich Village*

Sightseers gaze at the Statue of Liberty

• **Visit the site of the World Trade Center**. Whatever arises on the spot, parts will remain a memorial to those who perished on 11 September 2001. The day will linger in the memory of New Yorkers for generations to come (➤ 74).
• **Go to the 86th-floor observation level**, by elevator or up the 1,575 steps, of the Empire State Building. The city's tallest building offers fabulous art deco features to rival the stupendous views (➤ 18).
• **Walk, cycle, rollerblade, jog or ride** in style in a horse-drawn carriage through at least some of Central Park, one of the world's largest urban parks and without which New York really would be a concrete jungle (➤ 16).
• **Walk across the Brooklyn Bridge** (➤ 35), a major engineering feat of the 19th century and providing wonderful views of the Financial District skyline from across the East River.
• **Take the ferry** from Battery Park to the 151-foot-high Statue of Liberty but prepare yourself for the lengthy queues and a long climb (➤ 25).

• **Go to a Broadway show** but do not pay full price; make use of the cut-rate ticket booths at Times Square (➤ 26).
• **Ride the Staten Island ferry** for the outstanding views of Lower Manhattan.
• **Hang the expense** and have a drink or dinner at Rockefeller Center's Rainbow Room (➤ 66).
• **Stroll around Greenwich Village** on a Sunday afternoon and take a snack in the heart of the area, Washington Square Park.
• **Gaze at** Monet's *Water Lilies* or Van Gogh's *Starry Night* at the Museum of Modern Art (➤ 24), even if you look at nothing else.

The Shaping of New York

Pre-16th century
Several Native American groups occupy the land that later becomes New York; most are of the Algonquin tribe.

1524
A Florentine merchant employed by the French, Giovanni da Verrazano, makes the first European sighting of what becomes New York.

1609
For the Dutch East India Company, Hendrick (Henry) Hudson makes the first navigation of the river which later bears his name.

1625
The Dutch East India Company found a trading colony, New Amsterdam, on the future site of New York.

1626
Dutchman Peter Minuit 'buys' Manhattan from a group of Native Americans for the equivalent of $24.

1664
British ships blockade the harbour, a prelude to a British take-over that sees New Amsterdam re-named New York.

1776
The Declaration of Independence made by American settlers; in the resultant war, New York is the last major British stronghold to fall.

1785
Following the formal ending of the War of Independence, New York becomes the first capital of the United States.

1811
A grid-style plan for New York's streets is approved by city planners.

1825
The opening of the Erie Canal links New York with the agriculturally productive American Midwest, strengthening its importance as the nation's major sea port.

1848
Famines in Ireland and Germany bring a mass influx of immigrants to New York, the first of a prolonged series of arrivals of people suffering religious and political persecution in Europe.

1868
New York's first 'El', elevated railway, opens.

1886
The Statue of Liberty is unveiled.

1898
The City of New York is created by linking Manhattan, the Bronx, Brooklyn, Queens and Staten Island under a single administration; with a population of 3.8 million, it becomes the second largest city in the world.

Painting of 19th-century immigrants by Ford Madox Brown

1904
New York's first subway line is opened.

1929
Years of soaring rises on the New York Stock Exchange end with the 'Wall Street Crash', plunging the world into the Depression.

1931
The Chrysler Building is completed, the world's tallest building until overtaken by the Empire State Building shortly afterwards.

1933
Fiorello La Guardia becomes mayor and leads the city's recovery from the Depression. Prohibition ends.

1964
Enraged by police tactics, African–American areas erupt into violence; Harlem sees six days of rioting.

1968
In Greenwich Village, the 'Stonewall riot' ensues as customers of a gay bar refuse to yield to police harassment; the start of radical gay activism.

Left: *the Chrysler Building*
Below: *David Dinkins*

1978
Mayor Ed Koch oversees the tax-breaks and low-interest loans that help make Manhattan buzz with new building projects during the early 1980s.

1987
New York's army of yuppies are scuppered by a major crash on the stock market.

1990
David Dinkins becomes New York's first black mayor.

1993
A terrorist bomb causes an explosion at the World Trade Center. Rudolph Giuliani is elected mayor.

1973
The opening of the World Trade Center once again enables New York to claim the world's tallest building.

1975
Years of expenditure exceeding income leaves New York on the brink of bankruptcy. A federal loan saves the city but leads to years of cuts in services.

1996
After years of failure and humiliation, the New York Yankees win baseball's World Series.

2001
Almost 3,000 die and the twin towers of the World Trade Center are destroyed, hit by two hijacked passenger planes.

11

Peace & Quiet

More information about these parks and reserves is available on the following numbers.

Greenbelt ☎ 718/667 2165

Clay Pit Ponds Preserve
☎ 718/967 1976

Jamaica Bay Wildlife Refuge
☎ 718/318 4340

Fort Tilden and Jacob Riis
Park ☎ 718/318 4300

Gateway National Recreation
Area ☎ 718/338 3799

Sandy Hook ☎ 908/566 2161

New York might appear to be the most concrete of concrete jungles, but there are many ways to escape the hustle and bustle of the city and discover the parks, protected wildlife habitats and even the beaches that lie within a subway, bus or ferry ride from the heart of Manhattan, mostly under the auspices of the Gateway National Recreation Area.

The hilly, bucolic interior of Staten Island holds some of the city's most diverse and accessible unspoilt land. Covering 2,500 acres, the pristine area known as the Greenbelt spans a variety of habitats including wetlands, woodlands, streams, rivers and parks. The Greenbelt can be explored on a network of foot trails linking many of the main sites of natural interest; hardy hikers should tackle the major one, the 8.5 mile Blue Trail. From horse-riding to guided hikes and nature talks, organised activities take place within the Greenbelt each weekend.

On Staten Island's southwest shore, the 250-acre Clay Pit Ponds Preserve holds pine woods and the many ponds created by the one-time mining of clay that now provide habitats for a profusion of wildlife.

Between Brooklyn and Queens, sheltered from the ocean by the long and slender Rockaway Peninsula, the marshy islands and shoreline of the shallow Jamaica Bay form the Jamaica Bay Wildlife Refuge, a major breeding ground for egrets and herons and an important stop-over for migratory wildfowl. Walking trails lead through the area and visitors should come armed with binoculars. Throughout the year, there are guided bird-watching trips and lectures.

The Rockaway Peninsula itself holds Fort Tilden, a decommissioned military base with a dune system running across its 317

protected acres. The intricacies of the dunes and the hardy vegetation they support are described on guided walks from the visitor centre. The centre also dispenses maps of the fort's numerous trails, including one to the 50-foot summit of a former gun battery, revealing a fine view over the peninsula.

Swimming is not permitted at Fort Tilden but determined bathers can take a dip off the mile-long beach at the nearby Jacob Riis Park and admire an outlook encompassing New Jersey, Staten Island and Coney Island. Seclusion seekers should be aware that on baking summer weekends, much of New York seems to have decanted to Jacob Riis Park or Rockaway Beach, a short distance east.

Though requiring more effort to reach, another promising section of the Gateway National Recreation Area lies on the northern coast of New Jersey with the 6-mile-long barrier island known as Sandy Hook. Housed in a 19th-century lifeguard station, the Spermaceti Cove Visitor Center provides general information on the region and is adjacent to the mile-long Old Dune Trail, an enjoyable hack through the coastal vegetation. Also within reach is a 1764 lighthouse of great strategic importance during the War of Independence and among the oldest operating lighthouses in the US.

Aside from the crowded summer weekends, Brighton Beach's Boardwalk provides a chance to sit and gaze over empty sands and ocean

Opposite: *in the heart of Manhattan, Central Park provides unexpected moments of tranquillity*

New York's Famous

*Few film-makers have
such an intimate
relationship with New
York as Woody Allen,
who has presented the
foibles of the city and its
citizens to worldwide
cinema audiences*

Woody Allen

Though born in Brooklyn, film-maker Woody Allen recalls
'being in love with Manhattan from the earliest memory',
and made his name on the early 1960s Greenwich Village
comedy circuit perfecting an angst-ridden New York
Jewish persona. Two of Allen's most acclaimed films,
Annie Hall and *Manhattan*, both feature New York strongly.

Rudolph Guiliani

Serving two controversial terms as mayor from 1994,
Rudolph Guiliani oversaw a massive reduction in crime and
a new look Times Square that raised New York's profile.
Despite much publicised personal difficulties, Guiliani's
reign was heading to a tame conclusion on 11 September
2001. His competent and dignified handling of the crisis
resulting from that day's attacks earned admiration around
the world, and even his many adversaries acknowledged
his achievement in guiding the city through dark hours.

Cornelius Vanderbilt

The creation of a Staten Island–Manhattan ferry service in
the early 1800s was the beginning of a transportation
empire that soon linked New York with much of Latin
America and the California of the Gold Rush, making
Vanderbilt one of the world's richest men. When he died in
1877 his fortune was estimated at $105 million.

Andy Warhol

With images of electric chairs and soup cans, Andy Warhol
became a guru of 1960s Pop Art by manufacturing art and
underground movies. A 1968 assassination attempt and
investigations into his financial affairs prompted Warhol to
adopt a less confrontational profile and seek more lucrative
outlets for his creativity. Adopted by high society, Warhol
produced portraits for $25,000 a time and became a fixture
on the party circuit. His later years saw few successful
projects, and Warhol declared 'getting rich is not as much
fun as it used to be', before dying in 1987.

Mrs Astor

Acceptance into New York high society has never been
easy and from the 1850s the legendary Mrs Astor
(Caroline Schermerhorn, who married into the prominent
Astor family) ensured that it was impossible even for the
self-made rich. The 400 people invited to Mrs Astor's
annual balls were regarded as the city's social élite, and
she famously asserted that they could not include anyone
whose fortune had not been inherited.

Top Ten

Above: *riding around Central Park*
Right: *Statue of Liberty*

1
Central Park

Central Park, a mighty rectangle of green, is the soothing bucolic centre of Manhattan's concrete jungle.

70B4

Between 59th and 110th streets, & Fifth Avenue and Central Park West

212/310 6600

Always open; for safety, visit only during daylight

Tavern on the Green (£££); snack stands

59th Street, 72nd Street, 81st Street, 96th Street, 103rd Street, 110th Street

1, 2, 3, 4, 5, 10, 30, 66, 72, 86, 104, Q32

Good

Free

Special events throughout the year

Filling 843 acres in the middle of Manhattan, Central Park evolved during the late 19th century as the visionary plans of Frederick Olmsted and Calvert Vaux – intended to turn a collection of pig farms and squatters' camps into a 'specimen of God's handiwork' – took shape. Creating glades, copses and rock outcrops, the landscaping also involved the planting of some 5 million trees and the digging of the sunken roads that render traffic crossing the park invisible. Fifth Avenue became a fashionable address as the millionaires of the day erected handsome park-view mansions along the eastern side and took the air in horse-drawn carriages along its driveways. For New York's poor, the park provided much-needed escape from sweatshops and filthy tenements.

The park continues to mirror the full range of New York life. Whether jogging, rollerblading, strolling or walking the dog, Manhattanites of all kinds relish its green spaces – though in several isolated sections lone visitors can be vulnerable to crime. Pick up a park map from the Dairy, built in 1870 and first used as a place where traditionally attired milkmaids dispensed milk to mothers and babies, and plot a route to the numerous points of interest.

Cross the Sheep Meadow (which once really did hold sheep) for the Mall. Intended as a formally laid-out promenade, the Mall continues towards Bethesda Terrace and The Lake. Among the more recent additions to the park is Strawberry Fields, laid out as a tribute to British musician John Lennon and overlooked by the Dakota Building where he lived and was fatally shot.

Above: autumn brings blazing reds, yellows and oranges to the foliage of Central Park, seen here from its southeast corner

16

2
Chrysler Building

Even in a city packed with architecture of great merit, the Chrysler Building stands in a class of its own.

The definitive symbol of New York art deco and briefly the world's tallest building, the 1,045-foot-high Chrysler Building was completed in 1930 and remains one of the most distinctive features on the Manhattan skyline. Reflecting the car manufacturing business of the building's owners and the era's enthusiasm for machine-inspired design, many features echo automobile design. Architect William Van Alen made the first large-scale use of stainless steel on a building exterior, employed hub caps as decoration on each setback and made the attention-grabbing spire resemble a car's radiator grille, complete with outward-leaping gargoyles.

Once partly used as a showroom for new Chrysler cars, the lobby underwent a comprehensive restoration in the late 1970s. The work brought many features back to their original glory, notably the red-veined African marble walls and the elevators' plush laminated wood interiors. Although an observation level once existed at the base of the spire, there are now no public areas on the upper floors and visitors must content themselves with admiring Edward Trumbel's lobby mural depicting diverse images on themes of transportation.

The completion of the Empire State Building in 1931 robbed the Chrysler of its 'world tallest' status, though the title was only acquired in the first place through some slightly devious behaviour by Van Alen. The needle-like spire that tops the Chrysler Building's 77 storeys was secretly assembled inside the tower and pushed through the roof. In doing so, Van Alen outwitted his former partner, H Craig Severance, whose Bank of Manhattan Building (40 Wall Street), completed at just about the same time, would otherwise have earned the accolade.

✚ 43C6

✉ 405 Lexington Avenue

🕐 Mon–Fri 8:30–5:30

🚇 Grand Central

🚌 42, 98, 101, 102, 104

♿ Good

✋ Free

The upper floors and distinctive spire of the Chrysler Building

3
Empire State Building

✝ 43B5

✉ 350 Fifth Avenue

☎ 212/736 3100

🕐 Daily 9:30–midnight

🍴 Snack bar (£)

🚇 34th Street

🚌 1, 2, 3, 4, 5, 6, 7, 16,
34, Q32

♿ Good

✋ Moderate

❓ New York Skyride, a
flight simulator journey
above Manhattan

Perhaps not the best or even the best loved, but the Empire State Building is certainly the world's best-known New York skyscraper.

Conceived in the booming 1920s but completed in the gloom of the Depression, the Empire State Building rose at a rate of four-and-a-half storeys a week and was completed in just 410 days. By the time it was finished, however, the Wall Street Crash had left few companies able to afford its rents, despite the prestige of being housed in the world's tallest building, at a height of 1,250 feet (a further 222 feet was gained in 1951 with the addition of a TV mast). Through its early years, the building's only source of income came from visitors paying to sample the 80-mile or so panorama attainable on a clear day from its 86th-floor observation level.

While the views remain the major attraction, the building is a major contributor to New York's catalogue of art deco construction. From a base filling 2 acres (site of the original Waldorf-Astoria Hotel), the five-storey limestone and steel structure rises as a smooth-sided shaft with, unusually for the time, windows set flush with the wall. Inside, the three-storey lobby boasts marble walls and aluminium decoration, including the panels added in the 1960s depicting the 'eight' wonders of the world – the well-known seven plus the Empire State Building itself.

The building's 73 elevators include those designed to whisk sightseers to the observation levels at an astonishing rate of 1,400 feet per minute, and can take just seconds from the lobby to the 80th floor. The slower and much more arduous route, by foot up 1,575 steps, is undertaken annually in the Empire Step-Up race, usually completed by the speediest competitors in just 11½ minutes. Ordinary mortals take about half an hour just to walk down.

Sunlight catches the southern side of the Empire State Building

4
Grand Central Terminal

From an architectural viewpoint, there are few bigger, bolder or more beautiful places to buy a train ticket than Grand Central Terminal.

In 1939, as many people passed through Grand Central Terminal as lived in the entire US. The halcyon years of American rail travel saw Grand Central Terminal labelled 'the gateway to the nation' and a red carpet being set along a platform for passengers boarding the evening service to Chicago. As if to cement the terminal's metaphorical place at the heart of the nation's life, its name was (inaccurately) used as the title of a popular radio soap opera, Grand Central Station, first broadcast in 1937. Long-distance services no longer use the terminal and it is mostly commuters who can be found queuing at the ticket booths inside the magnificent Main Concourse.

Said to be the largest room in the world, the Main Concourse measures 375 feet by 120 feet and enjoys a *beaux-arts* form allegedly modelled on the Paris Opera. Above, a 125-foot-high vaulted ceiling is decorated by artist Paul Helleu's interpretation of the zodiac constellations. Although architects Warren and Wetmore take credit for the Main Concourse, much of the terminal's design, including the innovative split-level concept, is thought to be the work of another architectural firm, Reed and Stem.

Facing Park Avenue, the terminal's main entrance is a slightly overbearing triumphal arch topped by sculptured Roman deities draped around an American eagle and arranged over a 13-foot-diameter clock. Close by is a bronze likeness of transportation mogul Cornelius Vanderbilt, who owned the land on which the terminal stands.

Grand Central Terminal's Main Concourse

🕂 43C6

✉ 42nd Street & Lexington Avenue

🕐 Always open

🍴 Various restaurants (££–£££), cafés and snack stands (£–££)

🚇 Grand Central

🚌 1, 2, 3, 4, 5, 42, 98, 101, 102, 104, Q32

♿ Good

✋ Free

❓ Guided tours Wed 12:30 from Information desk on Main Concourse
☎ 212/697 1245

19

5
Greenwich Village

*The cafés, restaurants and bars of culturally
vibrant Greenwich Village are a major
element in Manhattan social life.*

*A stroll through
Greenwich Village reveals
every kind of shop*

30A2

Bordered by 14th
Street, Hudson Street,
Broadway and Houston
Street

W 14th Street or
Christopher Street

1, 2, 3, 5, 8, 10

Created as a wealthy residential neighbourhood in the 1780s, Greenwich Village then marked the northern extent of Manhattan's settlement and served to keep the rich away from the diseases sweeping through the poorer social stratas to the south. As the rich moved on, their vacated brownstone townhouses became apartments for newly arrived migrants who swiftly established businesses. By the turn of the 20th century, Greenwich Village was an ethnically diverse and socially tolerant area, with the low rents that helped attract the creative and unconventional members of what was later lauded as the first American Bohemia.

John Dos Passos, Eugene O'Neill and Edward Hopper were among the locally based novelists, dramatists and artists that created Greenwich Village's cultural reputation. By the 1950s, Beat writers and abstract expressionist painters were gathering in the area's cafés, and a decade on, Greenwich Village folk clubs saw the start of the protest movement, inadvertently becoming launching pads for major rock stars such as Bob Dylan.

Gentrification raised rents through the 1970s and 1980s and Greenwich Village people today are more likely to be successful lawyers or publishers than striving creative types. Nonetheless, the haphazard streets are a delight to stroll, packed with unusual shops and lined by well-tended brownstones, many sporting 'stoops' (a flight of entrance steps introduced by 17th-century Dutch settlers to prevent flooding) attractively decorated by their occupants.

At the heart of the action is Washington Square Park, a *mélange* of skateboarders, buskers and onlookers, above which stands the triumphal Memorial Arch.

6
Guggenheim Museum

The architecture might overpower the art but fans of both will find plenty to thrill them at this landmark museum.

Frank Lloyd Wright's stunningly designed Guggenheim Museum has been a daring addition to the Fifth Avenue landscape since the late 1950s, its curves and horizontally accentuated form totally at odds with the traditional architecture all around. The innovations continue inside where, rather than being hung in room-like galleries, the exhibits are arranged along a spiral ramp, allowing visitors to start at the top and steadily make their way down.

Many New York millionaires lavished fortunes on art, but Solomon R Guggenheim differed from the rest by switching from Old Masters to invest his silver- and copper-mining wealth into the emerging European abstract scene of the 1920s. Guided by Baroness Hilla Rebay von Ehrenweisen, a larger-than-life champion of the new movement in art, Guggenheim acquired works by the major exponents such as Léger, Gleizes and Delaunay, and a spectacular stash of paintings by Vasily Kandinsky. With these works and others hanging on the walls of his apartment at the smart Plaza Hotel, Guggenheim set up a foundation in 1937 to promote public appreciation of abstract art that eventually grew into the present-day museum, which opened in 1959, ten years after Guggenheim's death.

Selections from the Guggenheim collections, which also include Klee, Mondrian, Braque, Malevich and Modigliani, are shown on rotation and share space with high-quality temporary exhibitions. A broader selection of art is displayed in the Thannhauser Tower, a 1992 addition with a permanent exhibit of the acquisitions of art collector and dealer Justin K Thannhauser. These include important pieces by Degas, Picasso, Van Gogh and Cézanne, and amusements such as Henri Rousseau's bizarre work, *The Football Players.*

70B4

1071 Fifth Avenue

212/423 3500

Sun–Wed 10–6, Fri and Sat 9–8; closed Thu

Café (£–££)

86th Street

1, 2, 3, 4, 18

Very good

Moderate

Lectures

An unmistakable feature of Fifth Avenue, the exterior of the Guggenheim Museum

7
Metropolitan Museum of Art

70B3

100 Fifth Avenue

212/535 7710

Tue–Thu and Sun
9:30–5:30, Fri and Sat
9:30–9

Restaurant (£££) and
café (£)

86th Street

1, 2, 3, 4, 18

Very good

Moderate (includes
admission to Cloisters
on same day)

Lectures, films

*Inside (right) or out
(below), everything about
the Met is on an
impressively grand scale*

Founded in 1870, this mighty museum is a vast collection of anything and everything of artistic value ever produced anywhere in the world.

More than deserving of its reputation as one of the world's greatest museums, the Met's contents exhaust visitors long before visitors exhaust them. Make use of the information center at ground level to plan your explorations and be selective. Art lovers can meander through galleries that chart virtually the entire course of Western art. Memorable contributions include Botticelli's ground-breaking use of perspective with the *Annunciation*, and wonderful landscapes from Turner and Constable. Rembrandts and five of Vermeer's 40 extant paintings dominate the Dutch galleries, while El Greco's powerful *View of Toledo* stands out in the Spanish selections. The Impressionist and Post-Impressionist galleries hold noted works by Cézanne, Gauguin, Renoir and Van Gogh.

The influential paintings of the Hudson River School and a series of period-furnished rooms highlight the increasing self-assurance of American art as the country evolved into an independent nation. Among the strong points are a dazzling stock of Tiffany glasswork and a special section devoted to architect Frank Lloyd Wright.

With 40,000 objects dating from pre-dynastic times to the arrival of the Romans, the Met's Ancient Egyptian section begins with a walk-through reconstruction of the Tomb of Perneb and continues with case after case of immaculately preserved original exhibits.

Ten galleries are devoted to Islamic art, documenting the spread of Islam through intricate handiwork. Thousands of pieces highlight the skills of 9th- to 11th-century craftsmen in Egypt, Iran and Syria, and there is an enormous collection of ceramics unearthed by the Met's excavations at Nishapur, a 10th-century centre of Islamic creativity.

Major assemblages of Roman and Greek art, Chinese and Japanese ceramics, medieval European art (which continues at the Cloisters, ► 38), European arms and armour, the art of Africa, Oceania and the Americas, musical instruments, plus galleries of drawings, prints and photography, and modern art, consume only some of the rest of this vast museum.

8
Museum of Modern Art

Probably the world's best repository of modern painting and no slouch either with regard to sculpture, film and video.

It is hard to credit today, but when the Museum of Modern Art (MoMA, as it is known) staged its first exhibition in 1929 the featured artists – Cézanne, Van Gogh Gauguin and Seurat – were not represented anywhere else in the city and were considered too risky by the Met. Nonetheless 47,000 people attended the exhibition over four months and, a decade later, the museum acquired its current site, a gift from the wealthy Rockefeller family.

As the new museum was being created, the outbreak of war in Europe caused many leading artists to leave Paris for New York, making the city the centre of the art world and setting the scene for abstract expressionism, the US's first internationally influential art movement.

Abstract expressionism accounts for some of the most noted holdings: Pollock's immense and spellbinding *One*, Rothko's shimmering blocks of colour, works by De Kooning, and Motherwell's *Elegy to the Spanish Republic*. European contributions include Van Gogh's much eulogised *Starry Night*, one of Monet's *Water Lilies*, Matisse's *The Dance*, Picasso's *Three Women at the Spring*, Braque's *Man With A Guitar and Woman with a Mandolin*, and Mondrian's *Broadway Boogie-Woogie* revealing the impact of New York's jazz rhythms and grid-style streets on the Dutch artist.

Some of these pieces may be exhibited in the changing Collection Highlights gallery. However from the late-1990s MoMA's chronological approach to its holdings, so large that only around 12 per cent could find space in the museum's galleries, was abandoned as the museum entered the new millennium. Now the focus is on thematic exhibitions: mixing artists from different times and cultures, with work spanning painting, photography, design, video, multi-media and installations. The change coincides with a major expansion of the museum expected to be completed in 2004.

✚ 70B2

✉ 11 W 53rd Street

☎ 212/708 9480 (recorded information)

🕓 Sat–Tue and Thu 10:30–6, Fri 10:30–8:30

🍴 Restaurant (£££)

🚇 Fifth Avenue, 53rd Street

🚌 5, 6, 7, 18

♿ Good

✋ Moderate (Thu & Fri 5:30–8:30 by donation)

❓ Films, lectures

Above: *canvases to intrigue fill the Museum of Modern Art*

9
Statue of L

The most potent and e
of the US as the land
is the landmark Sta

Nowadays it is strange to think
known worldwide was initially
Frenchman Frédéric-August Ba
above the Suez Canal. The pla
1871 on a visit to New York, the sculptor found the
perfect site for his torch-carrying lady – at the
entrance to the city's harbour. Equally surprising in
retrospect is the antipathy towards the project on
the American side following the decision for costs
to be shared between France and the US as a
sign of friendship and shared democratic ideals.

As the lady, formally titled *Liberty
Enlightening the World*, took shape in
Bartholdi's Paris studio, the pedestal – the
responsibility of the US – made slow progress
due to lack of funds, which prompted
newspaper publisher Joseph Pulitzer to mount
a campaign to raise money through small
donations. The finished statue arrived in New
York in June 1885 and Pulitzer announced that
$100,000 had been collected. The lady was
duly placed atop the pedestal and unveiled in
May the following year.

Ferries to the 151-foot-high statue leave
regularly from Battery Park. Arrivals face
a choice between a possible three-hour
climb to the crown – up 354 steps
moving only as fast as the slowest
person in the queue – or the slightly
shorter journey to reach the pedestal
level. Both options bring photogenic
views of Manhattan, but the real
pleasure is simply being able to
clamber around such a powerful
symbol. An excellent museum
records the statue's story.

70B1

Between Bro
Seventh A
42nd an

✚ ☒ 🚻 🚾

🍴 Cafeteria (£)

🚢 Battery Park

♿ Few

✋ Moderate

❓ Audio tours

*Originally intended for
Egypt: the famous
Statue of Liberty*

10
Times Square

If a single spot yells 'this is New York' to the world at large, it is Times Square with its towering, animated neon signs.

The nights are almost as bright as the days thanks to the colourful advertising that surrounds Times Square

A gathering place for hundreds of thousands celebrating each New Year's Eve and the heart of New York's theatre district, Times Square is a frenetic, gaudy and until the late 1990s rather seedy junction whose fame far outstrips its actual appeal. The immediate area fell into social decline after World War II, but a major campaign to rid the area of its prostitutes, drug dealers and street con artists, and to limit the numbers of porno cinemas and adult bookshops in its vicinity met with considerable success.

Designated a Business Improvement District under a nationwide scheme financed by a tax on local businesses, the square steadily became safe for tourists and legitimate businesses with a major new development of hotels, shopping complexes and office blocks, and the restoration of many historic theatres. Major retail franchises, a number of theme restaurants, and a never ending stream of sightseers now dominate the area, which is patrolled by an unarmed security force.

Times Square was originally Longacre Square, but acquired a new name in 1904 when the owner of the *New York Times* got permission to build an office tower alongside it. By the 1920s, the vibrant New York theatre district had become established on adjacent streets. Raised in the heyday of vaudeville, many of the plush theatres remain in varied states of restoration. Through the 1930s, the local section of Broadway became known as 'the Great White Way' for its immense electrically lit advertising hoardings.

What
To See

Above: *a familiar sight*
Right: *Atlas, Rockefeller Center*

Manhattan

Manhattan may only be a part of New York City, but as far as the world is concerned Manhattan *is* New York. For visitors from near and far, this long slender island is everything they ever imagined New York to be. Times Square, Broadway, Central Park, the Empire State Building, the Museum of Modern Art and everything else that defines New York to the world at large has a Manhattan address and entices travellers to spend day after day tramping its streets with a sense of awe and wonder.

Once acclimatised to the wailing police sirens, the cruising yellow cabs, the street food vendors, legions of office workers crossing the road as one, and the general commotion that fills many a Manhattan street, newcomers will find themselves steadily discovering another Manhattan: one of neighbourhoods with a village-like insularity harbouring undiscovered attractions on quiet residential streets.

'Never let the poor and destitute emigrant stop at New York — it will be his ruin.'

CALVIN COLTON,
Manual for Emigrants to America
(1832)

Manhattan

Simply put, Manhattan has the lot. All the shops, skyscrapers, theatres and museums that draw visitors from all corners of the globe to New York are located across this surprisingly compact and easily explored island. With round-the-clock energy and something exciting around every corner, Manhattan may not be for the fainthearted but does offer the first-timer everything they dreamed of. For seasoned urban explorers, Manhattan means endless opportunities to discover something new.

Site of hotels and major attractions, Midtown Manhattan is where many visitors will find themselves staying and spending much of their time. While this effervescent area could consume your whole stay, a short bus or subway ride reveals more of Manhattan. South lies Greenwich Village with a rich cultural legacy and a major concentration of restaurants, bars, nightclubs and unusual shops. Further south is SoHo, centre of the world art market during the 1970s. Much of Lower Manhattan is consumed by the Financial District, a global powerhouse of commerce and holding the shrine-like World Trade Center site.

The heart of Manhattan is filled by the gloriously landscaped Central Park, an essential stop. East of the park, the Upper East Side accommodates Manhattan high society in elegant townhouses and luxury apartments. Framing the park's other side, the Upper West Side holds the American Museum of Natural History, reason enough to visit the area. To the north, Harlem is split between a predominantly African–American populated central area and East Harlem, main home of New York's sizeable Puerto Rican community.

Looking across peaceful Central Park to the skyscrapers of Manhattan

MANHATTAN

Spuyten Duyvil C.

Bronx Park

Inwood Hill Park

Dyckman House

4 The Cloisters Museum

Fort Tryon Park

Yeshiva University & Museum

WASHINGTON HEIGHTS

Crotona Park

BRONX

GEORGE WASHINGTON BRIDGE

Morris-Jumel Colonial Mansion

Audubon Terrace

Yankee Stadium

SOUTH BRONX

Aunt Len's Doll & Toy Museum

Hamilton Grange

Strivers' Row

Alyssinian Baptist Church

Schomburg Center for Research in Black Culture

HARLEM

3 Grant's Tomb

Black Fashion Museum

125TH STREET

EAST HARLEM

Downing Stadium

110TH ST

Wards Island

UPTOWN

Hell Gate

Henry Hudson Parkway

Central Park

UPPER WEST SIDE

UPPER EAST SIDE

QUEENS

Metropolitan Museum of Art

Roosevelt Island

Lincoln Center

QUEENSBORO BRIDGE

59TH ST

Rockefeller Center

QUEENS MIDTOWN

2 Times Square

MIDTOWN

42 ND ST

Murray Hill

QUEENS MIDTOWN TUNNEL

LINCOLN TUNNEL

Garment District

Empire State Building

Flower Market

Chelsea

23RD ST

East Village

14TH ST

Greenwich Village

LOWER EAST SIDE

DOWNTOWN

WILLIAMSBURG BRIDGE

SoHo

Little Italy

CANAL ST

East River Park

HOLLAND TUNNEL

TriBeCa

Chinatown

MANHATTAN BRIDGE

World Trade Center Site

FINANCIAL

BROOKLYN BRIDGE

Wall Street

JERSEY CITY

DISTRICT

BROOKLYN

1

Battery Park

BROOKLYN BATTERY TUNNEL

Ellis Island Immigration Museum

Fort Jay

Liberty State Park

Ellis Island

Governors Island

Statue of Liberty

Liberty Island

0   1 km

0   1 mile

Upper Bay   **A**

What to See in Manhattan

AMERICAN ACADEMY OF ARTS AND LETTERS ✪

Forming part of a series of neo-classical structures around a courtyard (known as Audubon Terrace), an Italian Renaissance building houses the American Academy of Arts and Letters. These two organisations amalgamated in 1977 and are pledged to honouring achievements in the arts by awarding grants and prizes.

Free exhibitions usually feature a few of the many American writers, composers and artists among the academy's membership, and there is a permanent display of bold, bright paintings by Childe Hassam.

✚ Off map 30A3
✉ 633 W 155th Street
☎ 212/368 5900
🕐 Tue–Sun 1–4, Thu by appointment only
🚇 155th Street or 157th Street
♿ Few
🎫 Free

AMERICAN BIBLE SOCIETY ✪

Founded in 1816 to circulate the Bible 'without doctrinal note or comment' throughout the world, the American Bible Society is a non-denominational organisation that publishes the Bible in over 200 languages, including Braille and American Sign Language. In the course of its work, the society has amassed a formidable collection of historically significant Bibles, including a 16th-century Gutenberg Bible, pages from which form the core of the changing displays in the public galleries of the society's 1960s high-rise office building.

✚ 70A2
✉ 1865 Broadway
☎ 212/408 1236
🕐 Mon–Fri 9–5
🚇 59th Street
♿ Good
🎫 Free

AMERICAN CRAFT MUSEUM ✪

Pottery, textiles, furnishings and sculpture are among the displays of the American Crafts Museum. The museum has occupied this location since 1959, though the brownstone townhouse that originally housed the collections has now given way to a towering office block. Compiled from loaned pieces and selections from the permanent holdings, exhibitions are arranged around a cunningly designed series of inter-connected galleries that fill a three-storey atrium.

Such a space makes an appropriate setting for diverse and imaginative exhibitions. These have ranged from Frank Lloyd Wright windows to Venetian glassworks, state of the art origami, futuristic jewellery in stainless steel, aluminium and plate glass, and a showcase of 200 American designers whose handcrafted household objects included musical instruments, kites, teapots, kayaks, knives, brooms, a saddle, snowshoes and a split-cane fishing rod. Lectures, demonstrations and workshops are also a feature of the museum.

✚ 70B2
✉ 40 W 53rd Street
☎ 212/956 3535
🕐 Daily 10–6, Thu until 8
🚇 Fifth Avenue
♿ Good
🎫 Moderate

Left: the view from the Empire State Building

Dinosaur skeletons are among the most dramatic exhibits of the American Museum of Natural History

✚ 70A3
✉ Central Park West and 79th Street
☎ 212/769 5100
🕐 Daily 10–5:45
🍴 Snack bar (£), cafeteria (£) and restaurant (££)
Ⓜ 79th Street or 81st Street
♿ Good
👆 Moderate

AMERICAN MUSEUM OF NATURAL HISTORY ✪✪✪

Boosted by 19th-century New Yorkers' thirst for knowledge and by enormous cash gifts from the city's moneyed élite, the American Museum of Natural History was founded in 1861 and, with roughly 36 million exhibits drawn from every corner of the globe, is now the world's largest museum.

The fossil and dinosaur halls are not only places to admire five-storey-high dinosaur skeletons, but they also make the most of state-of-the-art exhibits exploring the origins of life on earth from the Jurassic period onwards. Other representations of immense creatures include a fibreglass blue whale, the world's largest mammal, which sits above the other exhibits in the Hall of Ocean Life and Biology of Fishes. Displays on humankind include three halls devoted to Native Americans and the peoples of Africa, Asia and South and Central America.

Alongside the museum, a steel and glass cube provides a striking transparent exterior for the Rose Center for Earth and Space. Inside is the Hayden Planetarium and a series of walkways and galleries with displays on astronomical subjects including a space show The Search For Life: Are We Alone, narrated by actor Harrison Ford.

✚ 30A3
✉ Audubon Terrace, Broadway at 155th Street
☎ 212/234 3130
🕐 Tue–Sat 9–4:30, Sun 1–4
🍴 Café (£)
Ⓜ 157th Street
♿ Few
👆 Free (charge for guide)

AMERICAN NUMISMATIC SOCIETY ✪

Unsurprisingly, money through the ages and throughout the world is the main subject of the exhibitions of the American Numismatic Society. The displays include an intriguing assortment of maps, coins and paper currency spanning 3,000 years from ancient Greece to the modern US. Adjoining galleries showcase substantial numbers of medals and other decorations.

Upstairs, the Public Inquiry Counter can answer questions on money-related matters, such as estimating the value of that unfamiliar item you may have found in your change.

ASIA SOCIETY ✪

The patronage of the wealthy John D Rockefeller III enables the Asia Society to show off an impressive horde of Asian art, including wonderful Edo-period Japanese prints, pre-Angkor Cambodian sculpture and 11th-century Chinese ceramics.

The broader purpose of the society is to promote greater understanding between Asia and the US. To this end, it hosts an on-going series of films, concerts, lectures and workshops on Asian themes. The polished brown granite building is fronted by an image of a Nepalese guardian lion.

🔢 70B3
✉ 725 Park Avenue
☎ 212/288 6400
🕐 Tue–Sun 11–6, Fri until 9
Ⓜ 68th Street–Hunter College
♿ Good
🎟 Moderate

Below: *enjoying the sunshine in Battery Park*

BATTERY PARK ✪✪

Providing 22 acres of welcome greenery on the edge of the Financial District, Battery Park also holds more than its fair share of New York history, some of the details of which are supplied by the texts affixed to its lampposts. Created in the 18th century, the park's name stems from the cannons that once lined State Street, now framing the park but previously marking the Manhattan shoreline. The park's Castle Clinton, site of the ticket booth for Statue of Liberty ferries, was completed in 1811.

🔢 43A1
✉ Bordered by Battery Place and State Street
🕐 Always open; visit during daylight
🍴 Snack stands (£)
Ⓜ Bowling Green
♿ Few
🎟 Free

BROOKLYN BRIDGE ✪✪✪

Completed in May 1883, the Brooklyn Bridge provided the first fixed link between Brooklyn and Manhattan and, with a total length of 6,775 feet, it became the world's longest suspension bridge. The twin Gothic stone arches that rise 272 feet give the bridge great aesthetic appeal, though the most memorable aspect is the view of the Manhattan skyline as you cross from the Brooklyn side. Walkers, roller-bladers and joggers regularly cross the bridge; in 1884 21 elephants did the crossing in a stunt led by circus owner P T Barnum.

43B1
Between Manhattan and Brooklyn
Always open
Brooklyn Bridge
Few
Free

CARNEGIE HALL ✪✪

With an intimacy that belies its international fame, Carnegie Hall was built with $2 million from the fortune of industrialist Andrew Carnegie and has been highly regarded ever since Tchaikovsky arrived from Russia to conduct on the opening night in 1891. Guided tours lead visitors around the horseshoe-shaped auditorium, its design modelled on an Italian opera house.

The adjoining museum provides a systematic account of the construction, and remembers many of the great artists who have appeared here.

70B2
154 W 57th Street
212/247 7800
Other than shows, interior only on guided tours
57th Street
Few
Charge; museum free
Guided tours Mon–Fri at 11:30, 2 and 3; museum Tue–Thu 11–4:30

CATHEDRAL CHURCH OF ST JOHN THE DIVINE ✪✪

This is the largest Gothic-style cathedral in the world (it covers 11 acres) and yet, astonishingly, is still unfinished. The cornerstone was laid in 1892 but wars, the death of the architect, changes in design and regular shortages of finance have all played a part in causing the building work to be carried out in fits and starts. The most recent period of construction began in the 1980s after a 40-year hiatus. Temporary exhibitions fill the various nooks and crannies.

70A5
1047 Amsterdam Avenue
212/316 7540
Daily 7–7 Jul and Aug, 7–6 Sep–Jun
Cathedral Parkway
Good
Free

CENTRAL PARK (▶ 16, TOP TEN)

Left: *rose window of the Cathedral Church of St John the Divine*
Opposite: *Brooklyn Bridge*

Though primarily known for its list of famous and infamous guests, the Chelsea Hotel also boasts intricate 1880s wrought-iron grilles on its balconies

 43A/B5
✉ East of Fifth Avenue between 14th and 34th streets
☎ 212/744 2080
🕐 Call for hours
Ⓜ 23rd Street
♿ Good
🎟 Moderate

CHELSEA

The heart of Chelsea is around the junction of 23rd Street and Eighth Avenue, busy with shops, restaurants and art galleries since a 1990s regeneration made it one of Manhattan's most energetic neighbourhoods. On Chelsea's western edge, many former warehouses were converted into viewing spaces for the work of new artists, making the area a major showplace for emerging art. In the same section, four early-1900s cruise-ship docks have been redeveloped as Chelsea Piers, offering sports activities, dining and shopping, beside the Hudson River.

✚ 43B5
✉ 222 W 23rd Street
☎ 212/243 3700
🕐 Lobby always open
Ⓜ 23rd Street
♿ Few
🎟 Free

CHELSEA HOTEL

The Chelsea Hotel has played an important role in New York cultural life, providing accommodation for artistic and literary notables since opening in 1905. Featured in Andy Warhol's movie *Chelsea Girls* in the 1960s, the hotel also earned a place in punk rock history as the venue of Sid Vicious's alleged murder of his girlfriend. The hotel's lobby is strewn with artworks from former guests.

✚ 43B2
✉ Loosely bordered by Broadway, Bowery, Grand and Worth streets
Ⓜ Canal Street

CHINATOWN

An estimated 150,000 people, mostly Chinese but also Vietnamese, Cambodians and Laotians, live in the tight-knit streets of Chinatown, lined by restaurants, herbalists shops and stalls laden with exotic foodstuffs. Chinatown became established during the 1890s but began expanding beyond its traditional boundaries when the easing of immigration restrictions in the 1960s brought a major influx of settlers from Hong Kong and Taiwan. Numerous banks and busy stores reflect the economic vibrancy of the area.

CHRYSLER BUILDING (► 17, TOP TEN)

A Walk Around Chinatown

This flourishing ethnic neighbourhood, greatly expanded by increased Asian immigration since the 1960s, is one of the largest Asian communities outside Asia and one of Manhattan's most densely populated quarters.

Walk south along Mulberry Street from Canal Street.

The crowds and market stalls along Canal Street are an indication that you are approaching the heart of Chinatown. Call into the Museum of Chinese in the Americas (➤ 59).

South of the museum is Columbus Park, a rare instance of greenery in Chinatown. The park occupies the site of the notorious slum known as Five Points; Al Capone was just one who began a career in crime here. To the right, the Criminal Court Building overlooks the park.

Continue south along Mulberry Street and turn left along Park Street.

On the corner of Park and Mott streets, the Church of the Transfiguration predates Chinatown, erected in the early 1800s.

Turn right along Mott Street to Chatham Square.

Directly across the square is the 17th-century First Shearith Israel Cemetery, Manhattan's oldest Jewish graveyard.

Turn left across Chatham Square and left into Doyers Street.

Lined by restaurants, Doyers Street terminates at Pell Street, first rounding the bend which provided an ambush point during the early 20th-century battles between the rival Chinese–American secret societies known as Tongs.

Turn right along Pell Street to the corner with Bowery.

At 18 Bowery, the Edward Mooney House was completed in 1789 and is the oldest surviving Federal-style house in Manhattan.

Turn left from Bowery into Canal Street.

Distance
1 mile

Time
2–4 hours

Start/end point
Canal Street
✚ 43A3

Lunch
Joe's Shanghai (➤ 92)

One of Chinatown's brightly decorated shopping centres

37

43A2
Broadway at Murray Street
212/788 3000
Mon–Fri 9–4
City Hall
Few
Free

30A4
Fort Tryon Park, Washington Heights
212/923 3700
Tue–Sun 9:30–4:45 Nov–Feb; 9:30–5:15 Mar–Oct
190th Street
Good
Moderate

70A6
114th–120th streets between Amsterdam Avenue and Broadway
212/854 1754
Visit during daylight hours
116th Street
Good
Free

CITY HALL

When designed in 1803, City Hall was intended to mark the northern edge of Manhattan, but nine years later at the time of its completion, it was already engulfed by fast-expanding New York. Raised in a mixture of Federal and French Renaissance styles, the dainty building retains its civic role but its form seems entirely incongruous with the modern metropolis. Inside, counsellors go about their business and temporary exhibitions document various aspects of city history.

THE CLOISTERS

Medieval European monastic buildings might be the last thing anyone would expect to find in Manhattan, but the Cloisters are exactly that. Assembled on a site overlooking the Hudson River, these bits and pieces of French and Spanish monasteries collected in the early 1900s now showcase the Metropolitan Museum of Art's medieval holdings. The contents are a feast of 12th- to 16th-century creativity, but the show-stealer is the setting, with splendid views and an atmosphere much removed from the daily bustle of the city.

COLUMBIA UNIVERSITY

The British king George II founded Columbia University in 1754, since when it has steadily moved northwards across Manhattan, arriving at its present site in 1897. The predominantly red-brick campus buildings, reflecting turn-of-the-century American collegiate architecture, are grouped around compact plazas.

Inside the Low Library (based on Rome's Pantheon), the heart of the complex, are displays tracing the history of the university, one of the richest in the US thanks in part to owning the Midtown Manhattan land on which Rockefeller Center now stands.

COOPER-HEWITT NATIONAL DESIGN MUSEUM ✪✪✪

The museum, housed in the luxuriously appointed former mansion of steel mogul Andrew Carnegie, explores many diverse facets of art and design with outstanding temporary shows. Ceramics, wall coverings, textiles, drawings and prints form the bulk of the museum's stock of 250,000 pieces and the basis of most of the themed exhibitions. The collection began with the oddments the three Hewitt sisters picked up on a visit to London in 1897.

🗺 70B4
✉ 2 E 91st Street
☎ 212/849 8400
🕐 Tue 10–9, Wed–Sat 10–5, Sun noon–5
🍴 Café (£)
🚇 86th or 96th Street
🚻 Few
👐 Moderate

DAILY NEWS BUILDING ✪

Better known to cinema-goers as the home of the Daily Planet and mild-mannered Clark Kent, alter ego of Superman, the Daily News Building is the base of the *Daily News* newspaper. Alongside an immense globe and a weather-measuring exhibit, the lobby displays some memorable front pages.

The architect of the building was Raymond Hood, a seminal figure in the creation of the New York skyscraper.

🗺 Off map 70C1
✉ 220 E 42nd Street
🕐 Lobby always open
🚇 42nd Street–Grand Central
👐 Good
🎟 Free

DAKOTA BUILDING ✪

Destined to be remembered by the world as the place where ex-Beatle John Lennon was fatally shot in 1980, the Dakota Building had nonetheless already earned a place in the annals of New York history by being one of the city's first purpose-built luxury apartment blocks. Raised in the 1880s, the Dakota steadily attracted the rich and famous to reside within its intensely Gothic façade, and remains a prestigious address.

🗺 70A3
✉ 1 W 72nd Street
🕐 Private residence; view from street only
🚇 72nd Street

Opposite: *the Alma Mater statue at Columbia University*
Left: *the Dakota Building*

39

EAST HARLEM ✪

30A3

Loosely north of 105th Street & east of Fifth Avenue

110th Street or 116th Street

Since the 1920s, East Harlem has been the main base of the New York's Puerto Rican population and known locally as 'El Barrio'. Puerto Ricans' holding of US citizenship, plus the start of low-cost flights between the Caribbean island and New York in the 1950s, helped the city's Puerto Rican population expand to around 600,000.

The centre of activity is between 110th and 116th streets on Park Avenue, where the stalls of La Marqueta (the Market) proffer sugar cane, yams and papaya, and other culinary delights of the island, while ghettoblasters send the sounds of salsa reverberating into the air. Although predominantly Puerto Rican, Cubans and Dominicans, and others from Latin America, also figure among the Spanish-speaking population.

EAST VILLAGE ✪✪

30A2

Loosely bordered by Fourth Avenue, Bowery, First Avenue, 14th and Houston streets

Astor Place

Unorthodox lifestyles, unconventional beliefs and uncompromising modes of dress have long been part of the East Village (named for being directly east of Greenwich Village). Leon Trotsky propagated Bolshevik revolutionary views from a basement printing press here in the 1910s, Beat Generation gurus arrived in the 1950s, hippies in the 1960s, and punk rockers during the 1970s. Although much gentrification is evident, black leather, nose rings and tattoos are still far from unusual street attire.

Within the East Village is the long-established ethnic pocket of Little Ukraine, and the more recently evolved Little India along Sixth Street, more a centre for Indian cuisine than residence.

Above: *one of the many exotic shops to be found in the East Village*

A Walk Around East Village

The arty and offbeat factions of the East Village, the heart of New York hippiedom in the 1960s, sit alongside Ukrainian churches and cafés, partly on the land of a 17th-century governor of New York.

From Astor Place, named after John Jacob Astor, one of early 19th-century New York's wealthiest men, cross to Lafayette Street.

At 295–307 Lafayette Street, the 1880s Puck Building was the original home of the satirical *Puck* magazine; an image of Puck stands above the entrance. Just south at No 425 is the brownstone Public Theater, the city's first free public library, and a noted drama and film venue since the 1960s.

Return to Astor Place and cross Fourth Avenue.

Consuming the plot between 8th and 9th streets is the Cooper Union Building, base of the philanthropic educational institution founded in 1859 by millionaire Peter Cooper; Abraham Lincoln was one of many luminaries to address public meetings here.

Cross Third Avenue and continue along Stuvesyant Street.

Peter Stuvesyant, for whom Stuvesyant Street is named, was a noted 17th-century governor of New York, then the Dutch settlement of New Amsterdam. His estate covered much of the present-day East Village and Stuvesyant Street is thought to have been the driveway leading to the governor's mansion.

Cross 10th Street for the Church of St Mark's–in-the-Bowery.

Stuvesyant's remains, and those of his family, now lie in the graveyard of the Church of St Mark's-in-the-Bowery (▶ 67). The church holds Sunday services but is mostly used for readings and drama.

Walk north along Second Avenue.

Second Avenue leads through the heart of Little Ukraine and holds the Ukrainian Museum at No 203 (▶ 71).

Return to Astor Place.

Distance
1 mile

Time
1–4 hours

Start/end point
Astor Place
✚ 43B3

Snack
Café of Barnes & Noble bookshop
✉ 4 Astor Place

➕ 70B5
✉ 1230 Fifth Avenue
☎ 212/831 7272
🕐 Wed–Sun 11–5
🚇 103rd Street
♿ Few
💷 Donation

EL MUSEO DEL BARRIO ✪

Striving to link itself closely with the local East Harlem community, El Museo del Barrio grew from a local school class into a museum devoted to the cultures of Latin America, particularly Puerto Rico. There is a small permanent collection of pre-Columbian artefacts, but greater prominence is accorded to many temporary exhibitions documenting facets of Latin American history and culture. Paintings, folk art or sculpture might be featured.

➕ 30A1
✉ Ellis Island
☎ 212/269 5755 (ferry and ticket information);
212/883 1986 (general information)
🕐 Daily 9–5, longer hours in summer
🍴 Café (£)
🚢 Ferry from Battery Park, via Liberty Island
♿ Good
💷 Moderate

Ellis Island: the main building holds the Museum of Immigration

ELLIS ISLAND MUSEUM OF IMMIGRATION ✪✪✪

Twenty million people from 120 ethnic groups became US citizens after passing through Ellis Island, the country's major point of entry during the peak period of immigration from Europe that lasted from the 1890s to the 1920s.

Examined for contagious diseases, signs of madness and quizzed on their work skills, most arrivals found Ellis Island a bewildering and frightening experience, particularly after a long and uncomfortable sea voyage, and some were forced to spend time living in the cramped dormitories before being admitted to the US (approximately two per cent were denied entry altogether).

An excellent gathering of exhibits and oral histories documents the emotions of the immigrants and goes some way to suggesting the chaos that prevailed in the arrivals hall, where 5,000 people a day once entered carrying their possessions and speaking little English but looking forward to a new life.

DOWNTOWN MANHATTAN

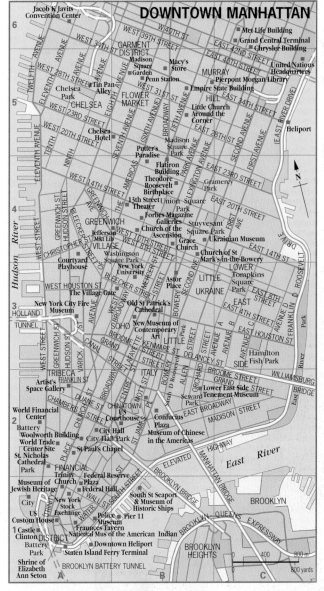

Jacob K Javits
Convention Center
WEST 39TH STREET
W 40TH ST
Met Life Building
Grand Central Terminal
EAST 42ND STREET
Chrysler Building
GARMENT
DISTRICT
EAST 40TH STREET
United Nations
WEST 34TH STREET
Madison
Square
Garden
Macy's
Store
MURRAY
Headquarters
WEST 28TH STREET
Penn Station
Pierpont Morgan Library
HILL
Chelsea
Park
Tin Pan
Alley
Empire State Building
WEST 31ST ST
FLOWER
CHELSEA
MARKET
Little Church
Around the
EAST 34TH STREET
Heliport
WEST 23RD STREET
Corner
EAST 28TH ST
Chelsea
Hotel
WEST 20TH STREET
Madison
Square
Park
EAST 23RD STREET
Putter's
Paradise
Flatiron
Building
Gramercy
Park
Theodore
WEST 14TH STREET
Roosevelt
Birthplace
13th Street
Theater
Union Square
Park
EAST 20TH STREET
GREENWICH
Forbes Magazine
Galleries
GREENWICH
Jefferson
Mkt Lib
Church of the
Ascension
Stuyvesant
Square Park
Ukrainian Museum
VILLAGE
WEST 10TH STREET
Grace
Church
EAST 14TH STREET
WEST 8TH STREET
Washington
Square Park
Church of St
Mark's-in-the-Bowery
Courtyard
Playhouse
New York
University
Astor
Place
LOWER
Tompkins
Square
Park
EAST 8TH
STREET
WEST HOUSTON ST
LITTLE
UKRAINE
The Village Gate
EAST 4TH STREET
New York City Fire
Museum
Old St Patrick's
Cathedral
EAST HOUSTON ST
HOLLAND
TUNNEL
SOHO
New Museum of
Contemporary
Art
Hamilton
Fish Park
KENMARE
STREET
LITTLE
ITALY
DELANCEY ST
SIDE
BROOME STREET
WILLIAMSBURG
Artist's
Space Gallery
FRANKLIN ST
GRAND
BRIDGE
TRIBECA
DUANE ST
CHINATOWN
Lower East Side
Tenement Museum
World Financial
Center
CHAMBERS STREET
US
Courthouse
Confucius
Plaza
Seward
Park
EAST BROADWAY
Battery
Woolworth Building
City Hall
Museum of Chinese
in the Americas
MADISON STREET
World Trade
Center Site
City Hall Park
St Paul's Chapel
St Nicholas
Cathedral
Park
FINANCIAL
DISTRICT
Trinity
Church
Federal Reserve
Plaza
East River
Museum of
Jewish Heritage
Federal Hall
BROOKLYN BRIDGE
QUEENS
City
US
Custom House
New York
Stock
Exchange
South St Seaport
& Museum of
Historic Ships
Pier 11
BROOKLYN
Castle
Clinton
Police
Museum
Fraunces Tavern
National Mus of the American Indian
BROOKLYN
HEIGHTS
Battery
Park
Downtown Heliport
Staten Island Ferry Terminal
Shrine of
Elizabeth
Ann Seton
BROOKLYN BATTERY TUNNEL

Hudson River

East River

N

0   400   800 m

800 yards

6   5   4   3   2   1

A   B   C

43

🕀 43A1
✉ 26 Wall Street
☎ 212/825 6888
🕐 Mon–Fri 9–5; closed
public holidays and
weekends during winter
🚇 Wall Street
♿ Few
🎟 Free

🕀 43A2
✉ South of Chambers and
Fulton streets
🚇 Bowling Green, Broad
Street, Cortland Street,
Fulton Street, Nassau
Street, Rector Street,
South Ferry, Wall Street
or Whitehall Street

🕀 43B4
✉ 175 Fifth Avenue
🕐 View from outside only
🚇 23rd Street

*A triangular building for a
triangular plot: Daniel
Burnham's Flatiron
Building. The clock in the
foreground, dating from
the 1860s, belongs to a
different building*

EMPIRE STATE BUILDING (▶ 18, TOP TEN)

FEDERAL HALL NATIONAL MONUMENT ✪

Federal Hall, in the heart of the Financial District, was completed in 1842 and is an accomplished example of Greek Revival architecture. Beneath an impressive rotunda, the airy interior holds assorted historical displays. One exhibit remembers the inauguration of George Washington as the nation's first president in 1789, an event which took place in the previous Federal Hall which stood on this site.

FINANCIAL DISTRICT ✪✪

New York's Financial District is the heartbeat of the US economy and a leading player in the global marketplace, yet many of the high-rise towers of commerce that litter the neighbourhood sit side-by-side with markers to a time when populated New York barely reached beyond today's Greenwich Village. Peek inside the 18th-century St Paul's Chapel (on Broadway facing Fulton Street) to see George Washington's favourite pew, and pay respects to Alexander Hamilton, the US's first treasurer, buried in the 17th-century graveyard of Trinity Church (on Broadway, facing Wall Street).

FLATIRON BUILDING ✪

The obvious way to maximise the potential of a triangular plot of land was to raise a triangular building on it, and with the Flatiron Building architect Daniel Burnham did exactly that. Completed in 1902, the 285-foot-high structure became the world's tallest building and was among the first in New York to use a steel-frame construction. This was a crucial element in the evolution of the skyscraper pioneered by Burnham 20 years earlier in Chicago. *Beaux arts* decoration on its limestone façade aids the building's lasting popularity.

A Walk Around the Financial District

All of populated Manhattan was once contained within the boundaries of today's Financial District, where historic churches sit amid a forest of skyscrapers and markers to two disasters.

From South Street Seaport (➤ 69), walk to the junction of Fulton and Water streets.

An unprepossessing model lighthouse serves as a memorial to the 1912 sinking of the Titanic.

Walk west along Fulton Street for St Paul's Chapel, immediately across Broadway.

Completed in 1766, St Paul's Chapel is the only pre-Revolutionary church in Manhattan. Preserved inside is the pew used by George Washington following his inauguration as the US's first president in 1789. Following the destruction of the World Trade Center (➤ 74) in September 2001, the chapel was covered with handmade memorials to the dead while the interior provided free food and solace to emergency workers. A block west across Church Street, new construction and a memorial occupy the site of the World Trade Center.

Walk south along Broadway to Trinity Church.

At the junction with Wall Street stands Trinity Church, completed in 1846 and the third church on the site. Inside is an excellent small museum; the graveyard holds the tomb of Alexander Hamilton, the US's first treasurer.

Walk east along Wall Street, turning right into Broad Street.

Wall Street's name derives from the barricade erected by Dutch settlers in 1653 to repel the British. At 20 Broad Street stands the New York Stock Exchange (➤ 62), the linchpin of the US economy; free tickets are available for the public areas from 9:15. Facing the exchange on Wall Street is Federal Hall National Memorial (➤ 44).

Distance
1 mile

Time
2–4 hours

Start point
South Street Seaport
✚ 43B1

End point
Federal Hall National Monument
✚ 43A1

Lunch
Bennie's Thai Cafe (➤ 94)

Looking along Wall Street to Trinity Church

43B4
62 Fifth Avenue
212/206 5548
Tue, Wed, Fri, Sat 10–4
14th Street–Union Square
Good
Free

FORBES MAGAZINE GALLERIES ✪✪

Larger-than-life publisher Malcolm S Forbes – his adventures included ballooning across the US and riding his powerful motorcycle at speed along Fifth Avenue – invested some of a fortune estimated to be worth $700 million on the eclectic collection of priceless artefacts and worthless curios that fill these galleries, within the building that houses *Forbes* magazine.

Encrusted with gems and made by jewellery-goldsmith Peter Carl Fabergé for the last two tsars of Russia, several Fabergé eggs are the treasures of the collection. Also exhibited, however, are a few of Forbes' 3,000 important American historical documents, 12,000 model soldiers in battle-ready poses and 500 model boats and submarines, some floating in a bathtub and viewable to the accompaniment of what purports to be the stirring sound of the Battle of Jutland.

43A1
54th Pearl Street
212/425 1778
Tue–Fri 10–5, Thu 10–7, Sat 11–5
Restaurant (££–£££)
Bowling Green, South Ferry, Wall Street or Whitehall Street
Few
Moderate

FRAUNCES TAVERN ✪

As ideas of revolution gathered pace in the British colony in North America through the 18th century, the Fraunces Tavern was a hotbed of subversive activity, a favoured meeting place for George Washington and his anti-colonial friends.

At the end of the Revolutionary War, Washington made a famously emotional farewell to his officers in an upstairs room, which is now the historical centrepiece of the present-day tavern, a re-creation (based largely on guess-work) of the original that offers pricey but cosy dining.

The General Grant Memorial, an ostentatious resting place for the military commander and 18th US president, Ulysses S Grant, and his wife Julia

FRICK COLLECTION ✪✪✪

Henry Clay Frick was perhaps the most detested of the self-made multi-millionaires who dominated US life in the late 19th century, although his outstanding art collection draws many to his former mansion where the relative intimacy of the setting is as enjoyable as the paintings, sculptures and decorative items themselves. El Greco, Titian, Rembrandt and Turner are just a few of the painters represented by exceptional canvases, while two rococo delights – Fragonard's *Progress of Love* series and Boucher's *Arts and Science* series – each occupy a room of their own. Other highlights include Gainsborough's *The Mall in St James's Park* and Rembrandt's 1658 *Portrait of a Young Artist – Self-Portrait*.

✚ 70B3
✉ 1 E 70th Street
☎ 212/547 0707
🕐 Tue–Sat 10–6, Sun 1–6
Ⓜ 68th Street–Hunter College
♿ Good
🎟 Moderate

GENERAL GRANT MEMORIAL ✪

Rising from obscurity to mastermind the battlefield strategies that helped the Union side triumph in the Civil War, General Ulysses S Grant became one of the best-known Americans of his time and was president from 1869 to 1877. A million people lined the route of his funeral in 1885, and he was buried in what was intended as a resting place commensurate with his status: a 9-ton granite sarcophagi within the granite hallways of this under-visited and oversized mausoleum.

✚ 30A3
✉ Riverside Drive at 122nd Street
☎ 212/666 1640
🕐 Daily 9–5
Ⓜ 116th Street
♿ Few
🎟 Free

GRACE CHURCH ✪✪

The grey-stoned Grace Church is one of the few things in Greenwich Village that suggests the European Middle Ages. Completed in 1846, the church was designed with a restrained Gothic Revival look, one of the earliest examples of the style in the US. The success of Grace Church helped Renwick win the job of designing the more prestigious St Patrick's Cathedral (➤ 67) and the first of the Smithsonian Institution buildings in Washington DC.

✚ 43B4
✉ 800 Broadway
☎ 212/254 2000
🕐 Mon–Fri 10–5:30, Sat noon–4; closed some Wed mornings
Ⓜ 8th Street–NYU
♿ Few
🎟 Free

Above: the former mansion of Henry Clay Frick, now holding the notable and popular Frick Collection

Gracie Mansion, the official home of the mayor of New York City

GRACIE MANSION ⭐⭐

Standing deep in today's modern metropolis, it is difficult to imagine that, on its completion in 1799, Gracie Mansion served its owner, Scottish merchant Archibald Gracie, as a country retreat. Gracie's elevated place in New York society, attained through the success of his shipping business, made the 16-room house familiar to many of the city's influential figures. But the War of 1812 decimated Gracie's trade and the house was sold in 1819.

The Museum of the City of New York was among the subsequent occupants until 1942, when the house became the official residence of New York's mayor.

GRAMERCY PARK ⭐

Enclosed by 19th-century brownstone townhouses intended to replicate some of the elegant squares of London, Gramercy Park is New York's only private park and entry is restricted to residents and guests of the Gramercy Park Hotel.

A stroll of the park's perimeter passes several notable buildings: the National Arts Club (15 Gramercy Park South) was occupied by state governor Samuel Tilden during his campaign against the notoriously corrupt Tweed ring in the 1870s; the Players Club (16 Gramercy Park South), marked by two ornamental theatrical masks designed by architect Stanford White, was an influential thespians' organisation founded by actor Edwin Booth, remembered by a statue in the park which depicts him immersed in the role of Shakespeare's *Hamlet*.

GRAND CENTRAL TERMINAL (➤ 19, TOP TEN)

GREENWICH VILLAGE (➤ 20, TOP TEN)

GRACIE MANSION

➕ 70C4
✉ East End Avenue at 88th Street
☎ 212/570 4751
🕐 Open for guided tours only (pre-booked): Mar–Nov, Wed
🚇 86th Street
♿ Few
💵 Moderate

GRAMERCY PARK

➕ Off map 43B4
✉ Between Irving Place and Lexington Avenue, bordered by E 21st and 22nd streets
🕐 Only open to local residents and guests of Gramercy Park Hotel
🚇 23rd Street
♿ None
💵 Free

A Walk Around Greenwich Village

While unmatched for restaurants and nightlife, Greenwich Village's artistic and literary past is also well in evidence on narrow streets lined with dainty houses.

Begin at Grace Church.

Designed by James Renwick, Grace Church was completed in 1846 in Gothic Revival style. The church marks Broadway's most southerly bend, a deviation in the otherwise straight route caused by a Dutch settler's refusal to let the road cross his land.

Walk west along 10th Street. Across the junction with Fifth Avenue is the 1840 Church of the Ascension. Continue south along Fifth Avenue.

At the foot of Fifth Avenue is Washington Square Park's Memorial Arch, bearing a likeness of George Washington.

Walk east along Washington Square North, then turn right into Macdougal Street and walk south.

Macdougal Street, south of Washington Square Park, holds numerous restaurants, including Caffè Reggio, number 119, in business since 1927.

Continue along Macdougal Street, turning right into Bleecker Street.

Bleecker Street is lined by shops and restaurants and is particularly good for evening strolling.

Cross Seventh Avenue and turn left into Barrow Street.

Barrow Street and its neighbours, such as Bedford and Commerce streets, hold many attractively maintained 19th-century homes.

Return to Seventh Avenue and walk north, turning right along Christopher Street.

At the junction with Greenwich Avenue stands the Jefferson Market Courthouse, completed in 1877 in a mix of Gothic styles. The building is now a public library.

Distance
2 miles

Time
1–4 hours

Start point
Grace Church
➕ 43B4

End point
Christopher Street
➕ 43A4

Lunch
Mama Buddha (➤ 95)

The Memorial Arch of Washington Square Park, designed by architect Stanford White and in 1916 briefly occupied by maverick artist Marcel Duchamps

GUGGENHEIM MUSEUM (▶ 21, TOP TEN)

HARLEM ✪

Many of the tens of thousands of African–Americans who arrived in New York in the late 1800s settled in brownstone townhouses erected in Harlem by developers anticipating an influx of affluent white residents from the Upper West Side. Instead, the neighbourhood became the US's most culturally vibrant black urban area.

Partly dilapidated, partly gentrified, Harlem holds landmarks such as the Apollo Theater (253 125th Street) and several churches where gospel singing draws as many tourists as neighbourhood faithful.

INTREPID SEA-AIR-SPACE MUSEUM ✪

Seeing service in World War II and the Vietnam conflict, the aircraft carrier USS *Intrepid* is now spending its retirement years as a museum. Both the vessel itself, its workings and wartime exploits comprehensively detailed, and the many exhibits arranged around its decks, explore the changing face of warfare and document the technological innovations spawned by it. Temporary exhibitions cover related themes, such as the role of women in the armed forces.

JEWISH MUSEUM ✪

An imitation French Gothic château erected in 1908 for banker Felix M Warburg provides an impressive home for the largest collection of Jewish ceremonial art and historical objects in the US. Among the enormous stock are household objects, coins and religious pieces dating back to the Roman era that help create a picture of Jewish life from early times to the modern day.

Many New Yorkers, both Jew and gentile, are drawn to the short-term exhibitions often presenting fresh perspectives on the Jewish experience.

HARLEM
- 30A3
- ✉ North of Cathedral Parkway; west of Fifth Avenue
- Ⓢ 125th Street

INTREPID SEA-AIR-SPACE MUSEUM
- 70A1
- ✉ Pier 86, W 46th Street
- ☎ 212/245 0072
- 🕐 May–Sep, Mon–Fri 10–5; Sat and Sun 10–6; Oct–Apr, Tue–Sun 10–5
- 🍴 Café (£)
- Ⓢ 42nd Street
- ♿ Good
- 💲 Expensive

JEWISH MUSEUM
- 70B4
- ✉ 1109 Fifth Avenue
- ☎ 212/423 3200
- 🕐 Mon–Wed 11–5:45; Thu 11–8; Fri 11–3; Sun 10–5:45; closed public and Jewish holidays
- 🍴 Kosher café (£)
- Ⓢ 92nd Street
- ♿ Excellent
- 💲 Moderate

LINCOLN CENTER FOR THE PERFORMING ARTS ✪✪

Part of what was the ghetto known as Hell's Kitchen and the setting for the musical *West Side Story* is now the multi-building complex of Lincoln Center for the Performing Arts. Since its 1960s completion, the center has provided homes for, among others, the New York Philharmonic, the Metropolitan Opera (the foyer of which is decorated by two immense Marc Chagall murals), the New York State Theater, and the celebrated Juilliard School for the Performing Arts, all grouped on or close to a central plaza.

🕂 70A2
✉ Broadway at 64th Street
☎ 212/875 5350
🍴 Various restaurants and cafés (£–£££)
🚇 66th Street–Lincoln Center ♿ Very good
🖐 Free to visit; charges for performances
❓ Daily tours; outdoor concerts in summer

LIPSTICK BUILDING ✪

In a city that sometimes seems entirely of towering rectangular blocks, the so-called Lipstick building dares to be different. Its nickname is appropriate, earned by its elliptical shape, its telescoping tiers and by its predominant colours of red, brown and pink. One of many buildings contributed to the New York skyline by veteran architect Philip Johnson and partner John Burgee, the Lipstick was completed in 1986.

🕂 70C2
✉ 885 Third Avenue
🕐 Lobby always open
🚇 Lexington–Third Avenue
🖐 Free

LITTLE CHURCH AROUND THE CORNER ✪

Formally known as the Church of the Transfiguration, this Episcopalian place of worship acquired its widely used epithet in 1870, when the pastor at a grander nearby church declined to conduct the funeral service of an actor and suggested that it be held instead at the 'little church around the corner'. New York thespians have looked kindly upon the daintily proportioned church ever since and several are remembered with their likeness in the stained-glass windows. The church sits behind a pretty and tranquil garden.

🕂 43B5
✉ 1 E 29th Street
☎ 212/684 6770
🕐 Call for times
🚇 28th Street
♿ Few
🖐 Free

Left: *Lincoln Center's Metropolitan Opera House*
Opposite: *well-tended brownstone houses in Harlem*

43B2

Bounded by Canal–Houston streets and Eliizabeth–Lafayette streets

Spring Street

LITTLE ITALY ✪✪

Today, only a few thousand Italians remain in Little Italy, an area that between 1890 and 1924 absorbed some 145,000 immigrants from Sicily and southern Italy and became awash with Italian restaurants and cafés. Over subsequent decades, Italians from the area became ingrained in the social fabric of New York life. Italian–American New Yorkers that grew up in Little Italy still regard it as a spiritual home, although increased prosperity prompted a mass movement away from the neighbourhood's tenement homes to more comfortable suburban living.

Undoubtedly the best time to visit Little Italy is during September's Feast of St Gennaro, when the compact area regains something of its effervescent past.

Not much remains of Little Italy, its shrinkage due to the steady dispersal of Italians across the city and Chinatown's expansion, but sufficient numbers of Italian-run cafés and restaurants line the streets of the compact neighbourhood to give an inkling of how the area might once have been

LITTLE UKRAINE ✪

While the East Village (➤ 40) embraces one counter-cultural phenomena after another, one section of the neighbourhood that has stayed relatively constant since the late 19th century is that known as Little Ukraine. Enforced conscription into the army of the tsar resulted in many Ukrainians fleeing their Russian-dominated homeland and settling here, establishing what, by 1919, was the largest urban Ukrainian community in the world.

A handful of restaurants specialising in *borscht* and *blintzes*, and a few craft shops offering *pysansky* (hand-painted eggs) reflect the East European character, while St George's Ukrainian Catholic Church, 16–20 E 7th Street, provides a community focal point.

🞖 43B3

✉ Centred on Second Avenue between Fourth and 14th streets

🚇 Astor Place

Food & Drink

Food and where to eat it is a major issue in New York, simply because competition is intense and New Yorkers are spoilt for choice. With some 4,000 restaurants in Manhattan alone, this is a city where you eat what you want, when you want, and do so at a price to suit all budgets.

Breakfast

A New York breakfast can mean dropping into a no-frills coffee shop for a substantial omelette with a seemingly endless choice of fillings, a plate of bacon and eggs or pancakes; in Chinatown it could mean a bowl of noodles or egg or chicken porridge. In more health-conscious establishments, breakfast can be a bowl of cereal and fruit served with a choice of quality teas and freshly–squeezed fruit juices.

One of the many colourful mobile food stalls commonly seen on Manhattan's streets

For a New Yorker in a rush, which on a weekday is most of them most of the time, breakfast can simply be coffee 'to go' and a Danish pastry, doughnut, or a bagel from the local deli. Some hotel restaurants serve breakfast, though this is rarely included in the room rate; some offer complimentary coffee and 'continental' breakfast, usually consisting of coffee or tea and a muffin and/or bagel.

Lunch

On weekdays, many restaurants offer attractively priced lunch specials, the cheapest generally around $5, and a lesser number of ethnic, chiefly Indian, restaurants present diners with an all-you-can-eat buffet. Most Chinese restaurants serve dim sum at lunchtime: bite-sized buns and dumplings filled with vegetables, meat or seafood ordered from passing trolleys.

Alongside outlets for American staples such as burgers, steaks and seafood served in generous portions (the basic fare of the many theme restaurants in and around Times Square), regional US cuisines such as Cajun, Creole, Southwestern, Soulfood and Tex–Mex are more widely available for both lunch and dinner.

International Cuisine

Reflecting the ethnic diversity of its population, the city also holds a whole range of international cuisines – Argentine, Brazilian, Chilean, Colombian, Chinese, Cuban, French, German, Greek, Indian, Italian, Japanese, Jewish Kosher, Korean, Mexican, Moroccan, Russian, Ukrainian, Spanish and Thai – to name but a few.

At the top end of the dining spectrum, New York's finest restaurants not only employ the world's best chefs but back them up with the top waiters and expensively designed interiors. The city has its share of food buffs ready to spend a week's wages on a meal in such surrounds, and most top-class restaurants require a reservation (sometimes weeks in advance) and formal attire.

Drinks

Deciding what to drink is almost as difficult as deciding what to eat. Diners serve coffee in endless free refills, but it can also be available as espresso or cappuccino in a variety of flavours and

Café Carlyle in the Carlyle Hotel – one of the places to eat in Manhattan

blends, and in regular and decaffeinated forms. Tea is growing in popularity, offered hot or iced and in a choice of flavours.

Most restaurants and bars serve a wide range of wines and spirits. Bars are increasingly serving quality beers, either brewing their own on the premises or stocking an excellent selection from the country's growing number of microbreweries, as well as importing lagers from Europe.

Customers choose their order at the counter of Katz's Delicatessen

LOWER EAST SIDE ✪

+ 43C3
✉ East of Bowery, south of Houston Street
Ⓜ Delancey Street

No part of Manhattan resonates with the immigrant experience more than the Lower East Side. From the mid-19th century through the peak years of immigration into the US, the high-rise tenements of the Lower East Side became crowded with successive waves of new arrivals: Irish, Germans, East Europeans, and the ethnically-varied Jewish settlers who made the Lower East Side the largest Jewish settlement in the world by the 1920s.

Nowadays, Orchard Street is noted for its discount clothing outlets and nearby Essex Street for its fruit and vegetable market. Much of this never-fashionable area's early buildings remain, though a number have been rased and replaced with largely unattractive, high-density housing blocks.

Cut-price clothing brings many a bargain-hunting New Yorker to this Sunday Market held on the Lower East Side

Reflecting changing patterns in immigration, many of the people who live here now are Spanish-speaking, mostly from Puerto Rico.

LOWER EAST SIDE TENEMENT MUSEUM ✪✪

+ 43B2
✉ 90 Orchard Street
☎ 212/431 0233
🕐 Guided tours only:
Tue–Fri every 40 mins from 1:20–4; Sat and Sun every half hour from 11:15–4:45
Ⓜ Delancey Street
♿ Few
💲 Moderate
❓ Guided walks Apr–Dec Sat and Sun

A cramped, rat-infested apartment shared with several other families was what awaited many arrivals to the Lower East Side in the 19th century – and for most it was far better than the conditions they had left behind in a troubled and oppressive Europe.

To get an inkling of early immigrant life in New York, visit this excellent museum which occupies an 1863 tenement building and is furnished to replicate the living conditions of the time. Companion exhibitions reveal diverse facets of local life and document the otherwise seldom acknowledged hardships faced by the Lower East Side's arrivals from Asia and Latin America.

MET LIFE BUILDING ✪

Looming high above Grand Central Terminal and infamously blocking the view along Park Avenue, the Met Life Building (formerly known as the Pan Am Building) was completed in 1963 and became the largest commercial building in the world, rising 59 storeys and offering 2.4 million square feet of office space. Bauhaus mastermind Walter Gropius was among the architects that created the structure which has an angled face that many say resembles an aircraft's wing.

- 70B1
- 200 Park Avenue
- Various restaurants (££) and cafés (£) on plaza level
- 42nd Street
- Good
- Free

METROPOLITAN MUSEUM OF ART (► 22–3, TOP TEN)

MIDTOWN MANHATTAN ✪✪

With its skyscrapers, department stores, high-class hotels, cruising yellow cabs, hotdog vendors and bustling office workers, Midtown Manhattan is for many visitors what New York is all about. Yet while the streets are teeming with humanity by day, after the evening rush hour much of the area is remarkably empty, save for well-defined areas such as the theatres district around Times Square (► 26).

The only deviation from Midtown's grid-style street layout is the former Native American trail much better known as Broadway, which weaves a path not only through Manhattan but continues 140 miles to the state capital of Albany.

- 30A2
- Loosely encompassing everything between 14th and 59th streets
- Any serving Midtown

MOUNT VERNON HOTEL MUSEUM ✪

On land purchased in 1795 by William Stephen Smith, an aide to George Washington, and his wife, Abigail Adams, daughter of John Quincy Adams, arose an Ashlar stone building which later became the Mount Vernon Hotel. Then on the fringes of the city, the hotel and its gardens were a popular day trip for wealthy New Yorkers until 1833. Eight rooms display colonial-era furniture and exhibitions on early 19th-century New York.

- 70C2
- 421 E 61st Street
- 212/838 6878
- Tue–Sun 11–4, Tue until 9 in Jun and Jul
- 59th Street
- Fair
- Moderate

A Walk Around Midtown Manhattan

Distance
2–3 miles

Time
2–4 hours

Start point
Times Square
➕ 70B1

End point
Rockefeller Center
➕ 70B1

Lunch
Lipstick Café (➤ 98)

Bisected by prestigious Fifth Avenue, in many ways this is the heart of New York City.

Start in Times Square.

Long a vibrant part of Midtown Manhattan, Times Square (➤ 26) and its immediate area has been transformed for the better in recent years. The completion of the New York Times building on the south side in 1904 gave the square its name.

Walk north and turn right into 44th Street.

The Millennium Broadway, number 145 W, is among the many new luxury hotels to appear in the area; filling a whole block the lobby provides pedestrian access to 45th Street

Continue east along 44th Street.

This route brings you to the distinctive Metlife Building (➤ 57), adjacent to Grand Central Terminal (➤ 19).

Walk north along Park Avenue.

On the right is the Waldorf-Astoria Hotel, renowned for pampering heads of state and other notables since the 1930s. The art deco features of the lobby merit a look.

St Bartholomew's Church, on the right, between 50th and 51st streets, was completed in 1919 by the celebrated New York architectural firm of McKim, Mead and White.

Decorative art deco features such as this one proliferate throughout the Rockefeller Center

Walk two blocks west along 50th or 51st streets.

Its main entrance facing Fifth Avenue, St Patrick's Cathedral (➤ 67) was completed in 1878 in modified French Gothic style. Inside, the chapels and shrines glow in candlelight.

Walk west across Fifth Avenue, continue along 50th Street and turn right into Rockefeller Plaza.

With the skating rink (winter only) to the left and the GE Building to the right, you are in the heart of the Rockefeller Center (➤ 66).

MUSEUM OF CHINESE IN THE AMERICAS ✪
A small but absorbing one-room documentation of the settlement of Chinese in the US. The main exhibits are a hotch-potch of family photos, items from Chinese-run businesses, and objects of symbolic significance from the homeland, although the changing temporary exhibitions examine many different aspects of the Chinese diaspora.

+ 43B2
⊠ 70 Mulberry Street
☎ 212/619 4785
🕐 Tue–Sun 12–5
Ⓜ Canal Street or Grand Street
🖐 Moderate

MUSEUM OF JEWISH HERITAGE ✪
Occupying a granite building topped by a distinctive six-tiered roof, the Museum of Jewish Heritage opened in 1997 and traces Jewish life and history from persecution in Europe to the creation of Israel and the growth of

+ 43A2
⊠ 18 First Place
☎ 212/509 6130
🕐 Sun–Wed 10–5:45, Thu 10–8, Fri 10–3
Ⓜ Rector Street
♿ Good
🖐 Moderate
❓ Lectures, films

Jewish communities, with excellent use of historic materials and interactive exhibits.

A diorama of the 1850s East River at the Museum of the City of New York

MUSEUM OF THE CITY OF NEW YORK ✪
This museum does its best to chronicle the story of the city's evolution from colonial settlement to international metropolis. Among the permanent exhibits are re-created interiors contrasting the spartan living conditions of the city's early days with the high-society elegance of later years, glittering silverware showing the skills of the city's 18th- and 19th-century craftsmen, and an extraordinary gathering of dolls' houses.

+ 70B5
⊠ 1220 Fifth Avenue
☎ 212/534 1672
🕐 Wed–Sat 10–5, Sun 12–5
🍴 Café (££)
Ⓜ 103rd Street
♿ Few
🖐 Moderate

MUSEUM OF MODERN ART (➤ 24, TOP TEN)

MUSEUM OF TELEVISION AND RADIO ✪
The museum is a fabulous resource for serious students of broadcasting and couch potatoes alike. Everything ever aired on US television or radio, including 10,000 commercials, is stored in the archives and made available from a computerised cataloguing system. Many items can be watched or listened to in private consoles, but most visitors will be content with the varied televisual selections screened each day and the choice of five audio channels carrying historic radio material.

+ 70B2
⊠ 25 W 52nd Street
☎ 212/621 6800
🕐 Tue –Sun noon–6, Thu noon–8, Fri noon–9
🍴 Café (££)
Ⓜ Rockefeller Center
♿ Good   🖐 Moderate
❓ Daily screenings of cult and classic TV shows

NATIONAL MUSEUM OF THE AMERICAN INDIAN ✪✪

43A1
1 Bowling Green
212/514 3700
Daily 10–5, Thu 10–8
Bowling Green
Good
Free

Although its holdings are slowly diminishing due to the insistence of many Native American groups for the return of their cultural treasures, the stock of this excellent museum, also called the George Gustave Heye Center, spans the diverse indigenous cultures of North, South and Central America. Among the baskets, quilts, pottery and other items of artistic, spiritual and cultural importance are some of the documents that paved the way for European colonisation of Native American lands. In a curious juxtaposition, the museum occupies an elegant *beaux arts* building that formerly served as the US Custom House.

NEW YORK PUBLIC LIBRARY ✪✪

70B1
Fifth Avenue at 42nd Street
212/869 8089
Thu, Fri, Sat and Mon 10–6, Tue and Wed 11–7:30
42nd Street
Good Free
Free guided tours daily 11 and 2, except Sun

The city's pre-eminent reference library and an architectural masterpiece, New York Public Library is guarded by a celebrated pair of stone lions, symbolising Truth and Beauty. Inside, the splendours of the design – such as the DeWitt Wallace Periodical Room and the wonderful mural lining the McGraw Rotunda on the third floor – are best discovered with the free guided tours. Various changing exhibitions in the side rooms, usually on themes of art and history, provide a further excuse to wander the magnificent corridors.

NEW-YORK HISTORICAL SOCIETY ⭐⭐

The hyphen in its name dates from the society's founding in 1804, a time when the city was spelled that way and when no other museum existed to receive the many bequests of wealthy New Yorkers. Consequently the society acquired a tremendous batch of art, from amateurish though historically important portraits of prominent city dwellers to seminal works by the Hudson River School painters and fine furniture from the Federal period. These items and much more fill several exhibition floors. Highlights include a substantial collection of Tiffany glasswork and the water-colours of John James Audubon's *Birds of America* series.

✚ 70A3
✉ 2 W 77th Street
☎ 212/873 3400
🕐 Tue–Sun 10–5
Ⓜ 81st Street
♿ Good
💲 Moderate

NEW YORK CITY FIRE MUSEUM ⭐

Fires were the scourge of early New York and so too, in many cases, were the fire-fighters. Before the creation of a municipal fire service in 1865, fire crews were privately hired and usually comprised members of rival gangs whose members fought each other before fighting the fire in anticipation of a reward.

The intriguing story of the city's fires and those who tried to put them out is told here over three floors with an entertaining collection of horse-drawn carriages, hose-pipe nozzles, axes, ladders, dramatic photos and New York's first fire bell.

✚ 43A3
✉ 278 Spring Street
☎ 212/691 1303
🕐 Tue–Sat 10–5, Sun 10–4
Ⓜ Broadway–Lafayette or
   Bleecker Street
♿ Few
💲 Donation

Above: *exhibits at the New York City Fire Museum*
Left: *the huge Reading Room of the New York Public Library*

NEW YORK STOCK EXCHANGE ✪

Within the neo-classical façade that overpowers Broad Street is the high-tech money market of the New York Stock Exchange. Wearing the brightly coloured jackets that indicate their particular job, brokers, reporters and pagers stride purposefully around the 37,000 square feet of trading floor, their successes and failures affecting the value of currency in pockets around the world. Visitors can observe the visually unspectacular activity from a gallery and learn something of stock trading's history and rituals in adjacent exhibition rooms.

📍 43A1
✉ Broad Street
☎ 212/656 5168
🕐 Visitors Gallery Mon–Fri 9:15–4; time-stamped tickets issued at entrance
🚇 Broad Street or Wall Street
♿ Good
💲 Free

OLD ST PATRICK'S CATHEDRAL ✪

Old St Patrick's Cathedral, completed in 1815, served the spiritual needs of the Irish population that inhabited the immediate area before the ethnic turnaround that transformed the neighbourhood into Little Italy.

The Gothic-style cathedral was seriously damaged by fire in 1866 and lost its place as the city's Roman Catholic see with the consecration of its far grander namesake in Midtown Manhattan (➤ 67) in 1879. Though unspectacular, the intimate interior makes for a few welcome minutes of respite from the city frenzy.

📍 43B3
✉ 264 Mulberry Street
☎ 212/226 8075
🕐 Call for times
🚇 Spring Street
♿ Few
💲 Free

PIERPONT MORGAN LIBRARY ✪✪✪

Financier J Pierpont Morgan was a major figure in late 19th-century New York life and lavished some of his immense fortune on manuscripts, rare books and drawings. Among the many treasures gathered here are Gutenburg Bibles, a Shakespeare first folio, a signed manuscript of Milton's Paradise Lost and handwritten works by Bach, Brahms and Schubert.

No less imposing, however, is the setting. Morgan's study was once described as the 'most beautiful room in America', but pales in comparison with the East Room, decorated by a mural-lined ceiling and a 16th-century Flemish tapestry above the fireplace.

<table><tr><td>✚</td><td>43B5</td></tr><tr><td>✉</td><td>29 E 36th Street</td></tr><tr><td>☎</td><td>212/685 0610</td></tr><tr><td>🕐</td><td>Tue–Thu 10:30–5, Fri 10:30–8, Sat 10:30–6, Sun noon–6</td></tr><tr><td>Ⓜ</td><td>33rd Street</td></tr><tr><td>♿</td><td>Few</td></tr><tr><td>💰</td><td>Moderate</td></tr></table>

POLICE MUSEUM ✪

The fabled mean streets of New York have produced more than their share of notorious villains, and many of them are recorded here, as are the officers who brought them to justice. The machine gun belonging to New York-raised gangster Al Capone is one prized possession, but this well-stocked museum also carries vintage handcuffs, truncheons, precinct logbooks and a terrifying assortment of weapons collected in amnesties.

<table><tr><td>✚</td><td>43A1</td></tr><tr><td>✉</td><td>100 Old Slip</td></tr><tr><td>☎</td><td>212/480 3100</td></tr><tr><td>🕐</td><td>Mon–Fri 10–5</td></tr><tr><td>Ⓜ</td><td>Fulton Street</td></tr><tr><td>💰</td><td>Donation</td></tr></table>

RIVERSIDE CHURCH ✪

Largely financed by John D Rockefeller Jr, the French Gothic Riverside Church has loomed high alongside the Hudson River since 1930. Intended to serve its membership's recreational as well as religious needs, the church has at times held schoolrooms, a gym, a theatre and even a bowling alley.

Originally Baptist but now interdenominational, the church's 392-foot-high tower houses the world's largest carillon, and has an observation level giving fine views across Manhattan's upper reaches.

<table><tr><td>✚</td><td>70A6</td></tr><tr><td>✉</td><td>Riverside Drive between 120th and 122nd streets</td></tr><tr><td>☎</td><td>212/870 6700</td></tr><tr><td>🕐</td><td>Tue–Sun 9–5</td></tr><tr><td>Ⓜ</td><td>116th Street</td></tr><tr><td>♿</td><td>Few</td></tr><tr><td>💰</td><td>Free</td></tr><tr><td>❓</td><td>Observation deck; Sun carillon concerts; guided tours after Sun service</td></tr></table>

Did you know ?

Corruption in public life was rife in 19th-century New York and extended into the police force. An 1892 newspaper investigation found that a $300 fee was required to become a patrolman, while $14,000 was the asking price for a precinct captain's job.

Opposite: the New York Stock Exchange, housed in a 1903 neo-classical building

In the Know

If you only have a short time to visit New York, or would like to get a real flavour of the city, here are some ideas:

10 Ways To Be A Local

If it rains, stand on the street trying to hail a taxi. If successful, New York belongs to you.

Ride the subway during rush hour and get out at the right stop. Crowds often make it impossible to see the station name and driver announcements can be incomprehensible; one trick is to count the stops.

If walking, shout abuse at passing drivers.

If driving, shout abuse at passing pedestrians.

Even if you are having a bad day, never tell a New Yorker that you would rather be somewhere else.

Visit Coney Island, then complain that it's not what it used to be.

Spend hours over Sunday brunch.

Although New York is safer than it was, always be wary of strangers on the street.

Do not expect a taxi driver to fully understand English, or have any idea of Manhattan's streets that have names rather than numbers.

Eat a bagel only if smeared with cream cheese; for a treat substitute lox (smoked salmon).

10 Good Places To Have Lunch

Anglers and Writers (££) Modest menu but great Greenwich Village atmosphere. ✉ 420 Hudson Street, Greenwich Village ☎ 212/675 0810

Chumley's (££) A prohibition-era speakeasy with great atmosphere and a reliable kitchen. ✉ 86 Bedford Street, Greenwich Village ☎ 212/675 4449

Emerald Planet (£) Inventively filled, healthy burritos. ✉ 2 Great Jones Street, East Village ☎ 212/353 9727

Gotham Bar and Grill (£££) The fixed-price lunch is tremendous value. ✉ 12 E 12th Street, Greenwich Village ☎ 212/620 4020

Mama Buddha (£) Excellent range of healthy Chinese fare. ✉ 57 Hudson Street, Greenwich Village ☎ 212/924 2762

Mandarin Court (£) A perfect stop for dim sum. ✉ 61 Mott Street, Chinatown ☎ 212/608 3838

Mars 2112 (££) Futuristic theme restaurant near Times Square. ✉ Corner of 51st Street and Broadway ☎ 212/582 2121

Maya (££) Top-notch

Mexican fare. ✉ 1191 First Avenue, Upper East Side ☎ 212/585 1818
Suzie's (£) Chinese eatery popular for its well-priced lunch specials. ✉ 163 Bleecker Street, Greenwich Village ☎ 212/777 1395
Victor's Café 52 (££) Cuban cuisine; vibrant atmosphere. ✉ 236 W 52nd Street, Midtown Manhattan ☎ 212/586 7714

10
Top Activities

Museums: there are many, and several are absolutely the world's best; allow ample time.
River: take a sightseeing voyage.
Walk: most New York neighbourhoods are best explored on foot; bring sensible shoes.
Theatre: probably the best in the world; read the media listings and go to whatever appeals.

Sit: on a park bench eating a cream cheese bagel.
Architecture: from Federal Period to International Style, New York has got the lot. Buy a specialist architecture guide and choose your favourites.
Art: the old stuff is in the museums but the galleries of Chelsea showcase tomorrow's hot names.
Eat: a different ethnic dinner every evening.
Shop: top designers, department stores, discounts outlets and secondhand bargains all feature here.
TV: if you really cannot resist, get a free ticket for the taping of a national show; details from the Convention and Visitors Bureau (☎ 1-800/NYC VISIT).

Above: *Macy's department store*
Right: *Park Avenue*
Top left: *elevated subway, Harlem*
Left: *second-hand bookstore, Broadway*

5
Best Views

- Towards Manhattan from the Brooklyn Bridge.
- Upper Manhattan and beyond from Fort Tryon Park.
- Lower Manhattan seen from Staten Island ferry.
- Observation level, Empire State Building.
- Manhattan from Roosevelt Island Tramway.

65

+ 70B1
⊠ Bordered by Fifth and
  Seventh avenues, and
  47th and 52nd streets
🕐 Always open
🍴 Various restaurants and
  cafés (£–£££)
📷 Rockefeller Center
♿ Good
💲 Free
❓ Expensive tours run by
  NBC ☎ 212/664 3700

ROCKEFELLER CENTER ✪✪

Bankrolled, as the name suggests, by industrialist John D Rockefeller Jr and spread across an 11-acre site, Rockefeller Center arose through the 1930s to become a widely admired complex of buildings that form an aesthetically satisfying whole, despite being designed by different architects.

Intended to provide a welcoming environment where people could work, shop, eat and be entertained, structures such as Radio City Music Hall and the RCA Building (now the GE Building) became noted city landmarks. The labyrinthine walkways are rife with eye-catching art deco decoration while the Plaza, overlooked by Paul Manship's golden Prometheus, provides a setting for outdoor dining during the summer and becomes a much-loved skating rink during the winter.

The scenic route to Roosevelt Island is with the Roosevelt Island Tramway, shown here as its cable car passes above the East River beside the Queensboro Bridge

ROOSEVELT ISLAND ✪

Roosevelt Island is a long, thin strip of land between Manhattan and Queens and a curious piece of New York that few visitors ever become aware of. Reached by subway or a short cable-car ride (the so-called Roosevelt Island Tramway), the island once held 27 hospitals providing for the terminally sick and mentally ill.

The ruins of the old hospitals (enhanced by avant-garde sculpture) stand on the island's southern end, while much of the rest has been developed since the 1970s as a car-free housing development by architects Philip Johnson and John Burgee. Initially winning many plaudits, the scheme has faltered due to insufficient finance and political will, but the island makes for an intriguing detour, if only for the stunning views of Manhattan.

➕ 30A2
✉ East River, between Manhattan and Queens
🚇 Roosevelt Island; also cable car from terminal 60th Street and Second Avenue

ST MARK'S-IN-THE-BOWERY ✪

The Episcopalian Church of St Mark's-in-the-Bowery is the second oldest in New York, completed in 1799 on the site of what was probably the chapel of the city's unpopular but influential late 17th-century Dutch governor, Peter Stuvesyant. It provides a useful local rendezvous for music and arts performances, as well as continuing its more traditional religious function. The now cobbled-over graveyard holds the bones of members of several generations of the Stuvesyant family.

➕ 43B4
✉ Second Avenue at E 10th Street
☎ 212/674 6377
🕐 Call for times
🚇 Astor Place
♿ Few
🎟 Free
❓ Poetry, dance and alternative arts events

ST PATRICK'S CATHEDRAL ✪✪

Nowhere else in Midtown Manhattan is there a sense of peace and tranquillity matching that found inside St Patrick's Cathedral, at its best when its interior is illuminated by candlelight. In a loosely interpreted French Gothic style, the cathedral was completed in 1878 by celebrated architect James Renwick; the twin towers that rise to 330 feet were unveiled ten years later. Despite being enclosed by modern high rises, the Roman Catholic cathedral, the largest in the US, retains its sense of majesty.

➕ 70B1
✉ Fifth Avenue at 50th Street
☎ 212/753 2261
🕐 Daily 7AM–9PM
🚇 51st Street
🎟 Free

SCHOMBURG CENTER FOR RESEARCH IN BLACK CULTURE ✪

A collection that began when a black Puerto Rican was told that African people had no history now comprises over 5 million items spanning rare books, documents, audio and video tapes, film, art and other artefacts documenting the culture of all peoples of African descent. A national research library primarily for researchers, the centre mounts strong temporary exhibitions exploring African and African-American themes.

➕ Off map 77D5
✉ 515 Malcolm X Boulevard
☎ 212/491 2200
🕐 Mon–Wed 12–5, Fri–Sat 10–5
🚇 135th Street ♿ Fair
🎟 Free (moderate for exhibitions)
❓ Special events, drama

70B2
375 Park Avenue
212/572 7000
Lobby always open
Four Seasons
restaurant (£££)
Fifth Avenue
Good
Free

SEAGRAM BUILDING ✪

Ground-breaking architecture is prevalent in Manhattan, but no single building is perhaps more influential than Mies Van Der Rohe's Seagram Building, completed in 1958 and widely regarded as the perfect expression of the International Style. Rising 37 storeys in glass and bronze, the Seagram Building also gave New York its first plaza, a feature that subsequently became common with high-rise development, sometimes being enclosed to form atriums. Walk into the lobby to admire the Philip Johnson-designed interior and the celebrated Four Seasons restaurant.

Off map 43A1
7 State Street
212/269 6865
Call for times
Bowling Green, South
Ferry or Whitehall Street
Few
Free

SHRINE OF ELIZABETH ANN SETON ✪

Elizabeth Ann Seton was canonised in 1975 for her philanthropic works – notably in education, caring for the sick and founding the Sisters of Charity (the first order of nuns in the US) in 1812 – becoming the first American-born Roman Catholic saint. This simple but well-preserved Georgian and Federal-style house was her home from 1801 to 1803 and holds a modest display relating to her life. Slightly ironically, Seton lived here prior to her conversion to Catholicism, which took place in 1805.

43B3
South of Houston Street,
between Sixth Avenue
and Broadway
Prince Street or Spring
Street

*In art- and design-
conscious SoHo,
imaginatively decorated
buildings enhance the
scene*

SOHO ✪

In one of the transformations that regularly regenerate Manhattan neighbourhoods, the previously derelict 19th-century factory buildings of SoHo became the centre of the world art market during the 1970s. A few years earlier, the well-lit spacious buildings had been attracting artists. As several new New York artists became internationally recognised, millionaire collectors arrived to snap up their works as investments and galleries opened on every street. The galleries remain, alongside chic clothing stores and restaurants, but most SoHo residents today are lawyers and media professionals.

SOUTH STREET SEAPORT

Through the 18th and 19th centuries, the centre of Manhattan's thriving maritime trade was around the area now consumed by South Street Seaport. This enterprising mixture of shops and restaurants beside the East River sits alongside a gathering of historic ships and nautically themed museums. While it fails to evoke the atmosphere of the past, the area and its numerous old ships – among them the 1911 *Peking*, a four-masted cargo vessel which can be boarded and toured – can enjoyably fill a few hours.

STATUE OF LIBERTY (▶ 25, TOP TEN)

THEODORE ROOSEVELT BIRTHPLACE

Theodore Roosevelt, the only US president to have been a native of New York City, was born to a prominent family at this address in 1858. Although the building of that time was demolished, what stands now is a detailed reconstruction of the childhood home of the nation's 26th president and contains many of the family's furnishings. A detailed chronology of Roosevelt's life outlines his numerous achievements, not least his acquisition of national popularity after leading the so-called Rough Riders during the 1898 Spanish–American War.

TIMES SQUARE (▶ 26, TOP TEN)

TRIBECA

Echoing the gentrification that transformed neighbouring SoHo in the 1970s, TriBeCa was, during the early 1980s, steadily colonised by artists who created living and studio space in buildings that once housed the city's poultry and dairy industry. Very soon, rising rents priced out the artists, and developers created chic loft apartments for well-heeled tenants. Serving the new population, TriBeCa's streets acquired fashionable restaurants, expensive boutiques and other services regarded as essential by the affluent and style-conscious New Yorker.

✚ 43B1
✉ Museum, Fulton Street
☎ 212/748 8600
🕐 Apr–Sep daily 10–6;
   Oct–Mar Wed–Mon 10–5
🍴 Numerous restaurants
   and cafés (£–££)
Ⓜ Fulton Street or
   Broadway–Nassau Street
♿ Good   Moderate

✚ 43B4
✉ 28 E 20th Street
☎ 212/260 1616
🕐 Wed–Sun 9–5
Ⓜ 23rd Street
🖐 Moderate

✚ 43A2
✉ South of Canal Street,
   between Broadway and
   the Hudson River
Ⓜ Chambers Street or
   Franklin Street

Above: *masts rise from South Street Seaport*

69

MIDTOWN AND UPTOWN MANHATTAN

Marcus Garvey Park

HARLEM

Riverside Church
Morningside Park
Columbia University
Cathedral Church of St John the Divine
CATHEDRAL PARKWAY
A C POWELL JR BLVD
ST NICHOLAS AVE
FREDERICK DOUGLAS BOULEVARD
MORNINGSIDE DR
CENTRAL PARK NORTH
LENNOX AVENUE
FIFTH AVENUE
MADISON AVENUE
PARK AVENUE
EAST 116TH STREET
EAST 110TH ST
Jefferson Park

BROADWAY
RIVERSIDE DRIVE
Riverside Park
HENRY HUDSON PARKWAY
WEST END AVENUE
AMSTERDAM AVE
COLUMBUS AVE
WEST 100TH ST
CENTRAL PARK WEST
Central
Harlem Meer
The Loch
The Pool

Wards Island
EAST RIVER DRIVE

El Museo del Barrio
EAST 104TH STREET
Museum of the City of New York
Mill Rock
THIRD AVE
SECOND AVE
FIRST AVENUE

WEST 96TH STREET
BROADWAY
UPPER
WEST 86TH STREET
Reservoir
Park
International Center of Photography
Jewish Museum
Cooper-Hewitt Museum
Guggenheim Museum
EAST 96TH STREET
EAST 92ND ST
EAST 88TH STREET
EAST 86TH STREET
Gracie Mansion
Carl Schurz Park
PARK AVENUE
LEXINGTON AVENUE

UPPER EAST SIDE

Children's Museum of Manhattan
WEST 82ND ST
Hayden Planetarium
WEST 79TH ST
American Museum of Natural History
New York Historical Society
WEST 72ND ST
Metropolitan Museum of Art
Delacorte Theater
Shakespeare Garden
Loeb Boathouse
The Lake
Hans Christian Andersen Statue
Strawberry Fields
Dakota Building
Sheep Meadow
Bandshell
EAST 82ND STREET
EAST 79TH STREET
EAST 75TH ST
Whitney Museum of American Art
EAST 72ND STREET

WEST
SIDE
CENTRAL PARK WEST
COLUMBUS AVE
BROADWAY
WEST END AVE
RIVERSIDE DR
WEST SIDE ELEVATED HIGHWAY

MADISON AVENUE
PARK AVENUE
LEXINGTON AVENUE
THIRD AVE
SECOND AVE
FIRST AVENUE
YORK AVENUE
FRANKLIN D ROOSEVELT DRIVE

Museum of American Folk Art
WEST 66TH ST
Avery Fisher Hall
Lincoln Center
Metropolitan Opera House
Damrosch Park
American Bible Society
Tavern on the Green
Holy Trinity Lutheran Church
New York State Theater
Dairy
Wollman Rink
Frick Collection
Center for African Art
Tempel Emanu-El
Zoo
Asia Society
EAST 66TH ST
Church of St Vincent Ferrer
Mount Vernon Hotel Museum
Rockefeller University
Bloomingdale's Store
Aerial Tramway
QUEENSBORO BRIDGE
West Channel

CENTRAL PARK SOUTH
EAST 60TH ST
EAST 59TH ST
Magic Town House
EAST 57TH ST
Calvary Baptist Church
New York Convention & Visitors Bureau
Carnegie Hall
New York City Center
Trump Tower
IBM Garden Plaza
Citicorp Center
EAST 55TH STREET
Lipstick Building
EAST 53RD ST
Museum of Modern Art
American Craft Museum
Equitable Center
Museum of Broadcasting
Lever House
St Bartholomew's Church
WEST 57TH ST
WEST 55TH ST
WEST 53RD ST
WEST 51ST ST

Passenger Ship Terminal
Radio City Music Hall
Rockefeller Center
St Patrick's Cathedral
Park Avenue Atrium
EAST 51ST ST
EAST 45TH ST
Met Life Building
Grand Central Terminal
Chrysler Building
United Nations Headquarters

Intrepid Sea-Air Space Museum
Pier 83
Circle Line Boat
WEST 45TH ST
Times Square
Port Authority Bus Terminal
WEST 42ND STREET
New York Public Library
EAST 42ND ST
EAST 40TH ST
MIDTOWN TUN

LINCOLN TUNNEL
Jacob K Javits Convention Center
WEST 40TH STREET
WEST 39TH STREET
Bryant Park
QUEENS

TWELFTH AVE
ELEVENTH AVE
TENTH AVE
NINTH AVE
EIGHTH AVE
SEVENTH AVENUE
AVE OF THE AMERICAS (SIXTH AVENUE)
FIFTH AVE
MADISON AVE
PARK AVE

A   B

0   400   800 m
0   800 yards

TRUMP TOWER

The New York of the [...] was the domain o[...] yuppie, and perhaps [...] greater role model exis[...] for the rapid creation [...] wealth than high-profile property developer Donald Trump. A heady mix of vulgarity, ingenuity and flamboyance, Trump Tower is a symbol both of the man and the decade's economic boom. The upper levels hold 263 luxury apartments while the lower six floors are a gathering of pricey retail outlets and restaurants. The interior decoration includes a five-storey waterfall.

[...]merous restaurants and cafés (£–£££)

 Fifth Avenue

Good

Free

UKRAINIAN MUSEUM

Though small and not widely known, the Ukrainian Museum in the area of East Village known as 'Little Ukraine' stores several thousand items of Ukrainian art, craft and culture, and displays some of them here. Usually displayed is a selection of traditional regional dress, numerous examples of the hand-painted eggs known as *pysansky* – a tradition that originated in pagan times to mark the arrival of spring and became linked with Easter in the Christian era – and changing exhibits that highlight various aspects of Ukrainian life past and present, both in the homeland and in New York.

43B4
203 Second Avenue
212/228 0110
Wed–Sun 1–5
Third Avenue
Few
Cheap

UNION SQUARE

Restyled in the 1980s, Union Square holds a popular farmers' market three times a week where fruit, vegetables, cheese and bread are sold from stalls. It is ringed by fashionable eateries: a far cry from the 1970s when years of neglect had turned it into a seedy drug dealers' haunt.

Created in the early 1800s, Union Square was originally at the heart of fashionable New York life but, as high society moved northwards, it became a focal point for political protest. By 1927, police had taken to mounting machine-gun posts on surrounding rooftops and, in 1930, no less than around 35,000 people protested here against unemployment.

43B4
Bordered by Park Avenue, Broadway and 14th Street
 14th Street–Union Square
Free

Above: *Trump Tower – 1980s aesthetics*

71

UNITED NATIONS HEADQUARTERS ✪✪

The United Nations has been based in New York since 1947, much of its administrative activity being carried out in the unmistakable Le Corbusier-designed Secretariat Building rising above the East River. Public admission is through the General Assembly building, which holds internationally themed exhibitions, and the ticket booth for guided tours, which provide an informative hour-long sweep through the UN's interior. Outside, the 18-acre grounds hold parks, gardens and abundant monuments.

UPPER EAST SIDE ✪✪

Few New Yorkers of good breeding would feel right living anywhere but the Upper East Side, the major residential neighbourhood of the rich and powerful since the 1890s when the top names began erecting mock-European mansions along Fifth Avenue, facing the recently finished Central Park. Comfortable brownstone townhouses sprouted on adjoining streets, now also dotted with smart apartment blocks.

In a parade of expense and pretence, Madison Avenue provides locals with antique shops, art galleries, boutiques, restaurants and dog-grooming specialists.

UPPER WEST SIDE ✪

The Dakota Building (➤ 39) set the tone for the Upper West Side and many more luxury apartment blocks through the late 1800s as residential development quickly filled the area between Central Park and the Hudson River. Decades of decline was halted during the 1980s with the arrival of yuppies seeking quality investments and liberal professionals fleeing the rising rents of Greenwich Village. Away from the quiet side streets, the commercial arteries hold a mix of furniture retailers, gourmet delis and fashionable ethnic eateries.

A Walk Along Fifth Avenue & Upper East Side

Long a byword for wealth and high social status, the Upper East Side is laced with 19th-century mansions, world-class museums and scores of prestigious shops.

Start in 65th Street.

The imposing 1929 Temple Emanu-El, on Fifth Avenue between 65th and 66th streets, has interior space for 2,500 people. The mixing of Romanesque and Byzantine styles is said to symbolise the meeting of East and West.

Walk east along 65th Street to the junction with Lexington Avenue.

The 1923 Church of St Vincent Ferrer holds impressive stained-glass windows.

Walk north to 67th Street and turn right.

Across 67th Street is a corner of the Seventh Regiment Armory, an imposing red-brick structure, its drill hall now used for special events. Ahead between Lexington and Third avenues is the crazed Moorish exterior of the 1890 Park East Synagogue.

Walk three blocks north along Lexington Avenue and turn west on to 70th Street.

Spacious St James Church (its entrance is on Madison Avenue) dates from 1884 but the handsome stained-glass windows and reredos were added in 1924.

Walk east along 70th or 71st streets to Fifth Avenue.

The Frick Collection (► 47) is housed in the former mansion of 19th-century industrialist Henry Clay Frick.

Walk north along Madison Avenue.

This section of Madison Avenue provides chic shopping opportunities for Upper East Side residents.

Walk east along 82nd Street to Fifth Avenue.

The Metropolitan Museum of Art (► 22–3) is entered by way of an awe-inspiring neo-classical façade facing Fifth Avenue, part of the museum's 1902 remodelling.

Distance
2–3 miles

Time
2–4 hours

Start point
65th Street
✚ 70B2

End point
Fifth Avenue
✚ 70B3

Lunch
Restaurant of Metropolitan Museum of Art (££)

Above: *out for a stroll in the Upper East Side*
Opposite: *the Secretariat Building of the United Nations rising up beside the East River*

73

70B3
945 Madison Avenue
212/570 3676
Tue–Thu and Sat–Sun 11–6, Fri 1–9
Café (£)
77th Street
Good
Moderate
Lectures, films

WHITNEY MUSEUM OF AMERICAN ART ✪✪

When the Metropolitan Museum of Art rejected her collection of American painting and sculpture in 1929, Gertrude Vanderbilt Whitney responded by creating her own museum, and with it continued her long devotion to supporting new American art.

Often controversial and devoting much of its space to relatively unknown work, the Whitney has an incredible collection of works by major names in US art such as Rothko, Johns and Warhol who are represented in the permanent collection. Three galleries are devoted to Calder, O'Keeffe and Hopper.

43A2
233 Broadway
Lobby Mon–Fri 7–6
City Hall or Park Place
Good
Free

WOOLWORTH BUILDING ✪

The world's tallest building for 16 years, the Woolworth Building – headquarters of the retail organisation – was officially unveiled in 1913 by president Woodrow Wilson who flicked a switch and bathed the building in the glow of 80,000 electric bulbs.

Leering gargoyles decorate the 800-foot-high tower but the real highlight is the lobby. Go inside to relish the blue, green and gold mosaics on the vaulted ceiling and the sculptured caricatures of the building's architect, Cass Gilbert, and its original owner, F W Woolworth.

43A2
Between Liberty, Trinity, Vesey and West streets

Right: the World Trade Center dominated the Financial District prior to September 2001

WORLD TRADE CENTER SITE

Almost twice the height of the highest buildings around them, the twin towers of the World Trade Center became a symbol of New York and of a US-driven global economy. On 11 September 2001, the destruction of the towers by hijacked passenger planes immediately claimed almost 3,000 lives, thousands more in the aftermath and brought increased fear and anxiety to the world. Following the attack, the site became a place of pilgrimage and neighbouring St Paul's Chapel was bedecked with handwritten tributes to, and mementoes of, the dead. New commercial buildings reflect the Financial District's determination to recover from the tragedy, but a permanent memorial is planned for the site to join Fritz Koening's *The Sphere*, a plaza sculpture that survived the attack, as a reminder of the fateful day.

> ### *Did you know?*
>
> *Gertrude Whitney, instigator of the Whitney Museum of American Art, was a wealthy (linked to the Vanderbilt fortunes) would-be sculptor who first displayed the works of John Sloane, Edward Hopper and other influential artists in a converted stable in Greenwich Village's Macdougal Alley during the early 1900s.*

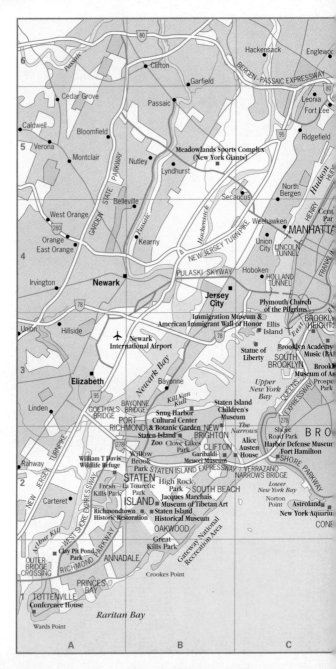

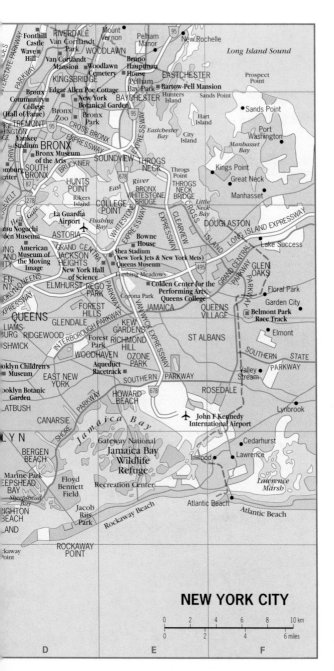

NEW YORK CITY

Excursions

Immersed in the varied sights and sounds of Manhattan, it is easy to forget that the 22.7-square-mile island is only a fragment – albeit by far the most famous fragment – of New York City, which also comprises The Bronx, Brooklyn, Queens and Staten Island. That these four regions are rather dismissively known as the 'Outer Boroughs' is indicative of their low esteem in the eyes of many Manhattanites and the short-shrift they usually receive from New York visitors.

However, while they do provide dormitory accommodation for those who live and work in Manhattan, each of the Outer Boroughs has fought vigorously to maintain its own sense of identity, history and cultural worth and each, in its own way, has something special to offer the curious traveller. Certainly a visit to one or a number of them will provide a fuller picture of the real New York City.

> *'A hundred times I have thought New York is a catastrophe and fifty times: It is a beautiful catastrophe.'*
>
> LE CORBUSIER
> *When the Cathedrals were White* (1947)

The Outer Boroughs

From sites such as Yankee Stadium and Coney Island that resonate deep into the heart and soul of New York, to the high-quality displays of the Brooklyn Museum and the American Museum of the Moving Image, the Outer Boroughs contribute much more to city life than most visitors realise. With Staten Island, they also offer a welcome chance to find rural pleasures within the borders of the great metropolis.

There may be just four Outer Boroughs, but in terms of character and actual places to see each is entirely different from its neighbours. Lying north of Manhattan directly across the Harlem River, the Bronx fills an expansive area and requires several subway journeys to cross between its major points of interest. Queens, east of Manhattan, is even more far-flung: mile after mile of sprawling, tidy suburbia that conceals a great deal of ethnic diversity and numerous pockets of history. Like the Bronx, a trip to Queens requires careful planning and adroit use of the subway system.

Lying east and southeast of Manhattan, Brooklyn is much easier to reach and in many respects the easiest to explore of the Outer Boroughs. An impressive number of attractions lie close to the Brooklyn Bridge, linking the borough to Manhattan and simple to cross on foot; though sensible visitors might prefer to save energy with the short subway ride. Linked to Manhattan by a regular ferry service, Staten Island guarantees a peaceful few hours of pastoral exploration and is well covered by easy-to-understand bus routes.

The elegant Victorian-style conservatory in New York Botanical Garden was inspired by London's Kew Gardens

Yankee Stadium became known as the 'House that Ruth Built', a reference to the legendary Babe Ruth whose joining of the Yankees coincided with the construction of the stadium

The Bronx

Spanning rundown areas such as the South Bronx, and comfortable residential areas, the Bronx tends to be neglected by visitors and New Yorkers alike. Nonetheless, with the Bronx Zoo and Yankee Stadium, the borough holds two of the city's major attractions as well as several minor ones, including the one-time home of author Edgar Allen Poe (East Kingsbridge Road) and the elegant 18th-century Van Cortlandt Mansion (Broadway between 240th and 242nd streets), built for a family prominent in politics and farming, now a showplace of English, Dutch and Colonial period furnishings.

BRONX ZOO ⬤⬤

The largest city zoo in the US, the Bronx Zoo holds spacious replicated habitats inhabited by antelopes, rhinos, elephants, snow leopards, monkeys, gorillas and many more creatures from around the world. Nocturnal species can be observed in the World of Darkness area which turns day into night and brings glimpses of foxes, aardvarks and bats going about their nightly pursuits. A 25-minute monorail ride provides an overview, and there is a children's zoo packed with furry creatures.

YANKEE STADIUM ⬤

Home of the New York Yankees baseball team since its 1923 completion, Yankee Stadium has seen tens of thousands of spectators thrilling to Babe Ruth and Joe di Maggio – and many less distinguished stars over the years – plus Pope Paul conducting mass in 1965. It now has a capacity of 57,000 (the stadium underwent a $100-million remodelling in the 1970s – its original cost was in the region of $2½ million), and its 11-acre site is scattered with memorials to Yankee greats.

77D5
Bronx River Parkway, Fordham Road
718/367 1010
Apr–Oct Mon–Fri 10–5, Sat and Sun 10–5:30; Nov–Mar daily 10–4:30
Pelham Parkway
Good
Moderate

77D5
Junction of 161st Street and River Avenue
718/293 6000
Baseball season Apr–Oct
161st Street–Yankee Stadium
Good
Variously priced match tickets

Brooklyn

Physically, only the East River divides Brooklyn from Manhattan but this so-called Outer Borough retains a distinct identity, in part a legacy of its origins as a self-governing city separate from Manhattan. In a mood of regional unity that followed the opening of the Brooklyn Bridge, the people of Brooklyn voted by a narrow margin to give up their autonomy in 1898.

Since then, the pride of Brooklynites has been greatly dented by a series of economic reverses, made all the worse by the inexorable rise of Manhattan. The demise of the *Brooklyn Eagle* robbed the borough of its daily newspaper and the closure of the naval dockyards, that had employed 70,000 people in round-the-clock shifts, came in 1966. But perhaps the most symbolic sense of loss to many was with the departure of the successful Brooklyn Dodgers baseball team to Los Angeles in 1955.

The popularity of the 1950s TV sitcom *The Honeymooners*, starring locally born actor Jackie Gleason, helped solidify Brooklyn's reputation as a working-class area of warm-hearted if unsophisticated souls, though the image was a misleading one. Brooklyn has been an ethnically diverse community since its earliest days, and among its present-day residents are some 2 million arrivals from Asia and Cuba.

Brooklyn enjoys a strong reputation for its cultural institutions, such as the Brooklyn Museum and the Brooklyn Academy of Music, and with Coney Island holds what many consider an historic icon of New York life.

Even the skyscrapers in Brooklyn Heights have an elegant charm

76C3
Eastern Parkway at Prospect Park
718/638 5000
Wed–Fri 10–5, Sat and Sun 11–6, first Sat of month 11–11
Eastern Parkway– Brooklyn Museum
Good
Moderate

BROOKLYN MUSEUM OF ART 😀😀😀

In keeping with the world-conquering attitude of 19th-century Brooklyn, the Brooklyn Museum of Art was conceived with no less an ambition than for it to be the biggest in the world. The exuberant *beaux arts* architecture that the revered New York firm of McKim, Mead and White created for the six-storey museum between 1897 and the 1920s suggests its elevated goal, although the museum was only partially completed to its original plan due to the waning financial support that followed Brooklyn's absorption into New York City. The museum's 1980s renovation was the work of celebrated Japanese architect Arata Isozaki.

Now the seventh largest museum in the US and in New York second only to Manhattan's Metropolitan Museum of Art, the Brooklyn Museum will easily consume several hours, if not a full day. The Egyptian collections alone are outstanding and include more than 500 items of stunningly decorated sarcophagi, sculpture and wall reliefs. Mosaics, ceramics and bronzes feature among the substantial horde of artefacts from ancient Greece and Rome, and 12 monumental reliefs from 9th-century BC Abyssinia form the core of the Middle East displays.

From more recent periods, a fine collection of paintings and period rooms highlight changing American tastes from colonial times onward. Among the canvases are one of Gilbert Stuart's iconographic portraits of George Washington, painted in the 1790s. Impressive works from the Hudson River School artists culminate in Albert Bierdstadt's enormous evocation of nature in *Storm in the Rocky Mountains, Mount Rosalie*.

Among the evocative studies of New York in the Brooklyn Museum is Early Spring Afternoon, Central Park, 1911, *by Willard Leroy Metcalf*

A Walk Around Brooklyn Heights

Tidy streets lined with brownstone houses and fabulous Manhattan views help make Brooklyn Heights one of the classiest neighbourhoods in the Outer Boroughs.

Exit from Borough Hall subway station on to Joralemon Street.

At 209 Joralemon Street, Brooklyn Borough Hall has been the area's administrative base since 1802 but its current Greek Revival form dates from 1851. On the other side of Joralemon Street, the Brooklyn Municipal Building was completed in 1926.

Turn right into Court Street and left into Montague Street.

Lined by shops and restaurants, Montague Street is the main commercial strip of Brooklyn Heights. On the corner with Clinton Street, the Church of St Anne and the Holy Trinity is a finely proportioned rendition of a Gothic church in local brownstone topped by a soaring spire. Finished in 1847, the church often stages musical and theatrical events.

Walk a block north to Pierrepont Street.

At 128 Pierrepont Street is the elegant home of Brooklyn's History Museum (➤ 84–5).

Return to Montague Street and walk west.

Before the opening of the Brooklyn Bridge (➤ 35), the western end of Montague Street held the departure point for a ferry service to Manhattan's Financial District, an excellent view of which can be found along the Esplanade (also known as the Promenade) running north from Montague Street and lined with inviting benches.

Follow the Esplanade north and turn right into Orange Street.

Immediately past the junction with Hicks Street stands the Plymouth Church of the Pilgrims (➤ 85).

Distance
1 mile

Time
1–4 hours

Start point
Joralemon Street
⊞ 76C3

End point
Orange Street
⊞ 76C3

Lunch
Andy's (££)
✉ 128 Montague Street
☎ 718/237 8899

A long-serving grocery store in Brooklyn Heights

BROOKLYN BOTANIC GARDEN ✪

Occupying a one-time waste dump, the Brooklyn Botanic Garden fills 52 acres with 12,000 plant species. Passing magnolias and cherry trees, the footpaths weave through lushly landscaped surrounds linking the various sections. Perennial favourites are the Rose Garden, Herb Garden and the exquisite 1914 Japanese Garden complete with pond, stone lanterns and viewing pavilion.

Inside the three-part Steinhart Conservatory are plants from the world's deserts, rainforests and warm temperate regions, while fans of bonsai will find much to admire in the C V Starr Bonsai Museum.

BROOKLYN'S HISTORY MUSEUM ✪✪

It is a measure of Brooklyn's strong sense of self-worth that as early as the 1880s this elegant and spacious red-brick building had been purpose-built to enable the local community to look back over its past. With a $5 million restoration expected to continue for several years many exhibits, which span 9,000 artefacts, 100,000 graphic images, and a lot more, all reflecting Brooklyn's history,

Above: *colourful vegetation threatens to overwhelm visitors to Brooklyn Botanic Garden*
Right: *Brooklyn Bridge at sunset*

will be shown in temporary exhibitions in various locations around the city

Be it the changing ethnic makeup of the city, the rise and fall of the naval dockyards, the opening of the Brooklyn Bridge, the creation of Coney Island, or the 1955 World Series-winning Brooklyn Dodgers, the museum details chapters of Brooklyn's past with an engaging clutter of memorabilia and photography, all bolstered by clear and elucidating texts.

NEW YORK TRANSIT MUSEUM

Housed in a former subway station, the New York Transit Museum holds the finely crafted art deco air vents and ceramic station nameplates indicative of the care that went into creating what became the world's second-largest mass transit system. Arranged alongside a platform, walk-through subway cars from 1904 to 1964 demonstrate stylistic changes and technological innovations that, despite what many of today's regular users might think, are proof that New York's mass transit is now more comfortable and efficient than ever before.

- 76C3
- 130 Livingston Street
- 718/243 8601
- Tue, Thu and Fri 10–4, Wed 10–6, Sat–Sun noon–5
- Boerum Place–Schermerhorn Street
- Good
- Moderate

PLYMOUTH CHURCH OF THE PILGRIMS

With seating for 2,800 people, the Plymouth Church of the Pilgrims, completed in 1850, became the best-known public meeting place in Brooklyn. The church was noted above all for the sermons of Henry Ward Beecher, resident clergyman for some 40 years and a popular speaker who promoted the abolition of slavery and women's suffrage, while his writings controversially supported Darwin's theory of evolution.

Although the church's barn-like interior can now hold only 2,000 people, it is highly evocative of the great gatherings of the past. Beecher, who died in 1887 (his later years dogged by allegations of adultery), is remembered by a statue that stands in the adjoining garden.

- 76C3
- Corner of Hicks and Orange streets
- 718/624 4743
- Call for hours; sometimes open by appointment
- Borough Hall or Clark Street
- Few
- Free

PROSPECT PARK

Manhattan's Central Park may be better known, but many Brooklynites regard it simply as a trial run for Prospect Park, laid out by the same design team of Frederick Law Olsted and Calvert Vaux through the 1860s. The 526-acre park encompasses lawns, meadows, streams and ponds, and provides the community with a bucolic space for jogging, strolling, picnicking, plus many special events throughout the year. In 1870, the park's main entrance gained the Soldiers' and Sailors' Memorial Arch, a triumphal marker to the fallen of the Civil War.

- 76C3
- 450 Flatbush Avenue
- 718/965 8951
- Visit during daylight hours
- Grand Army Plaza
- Few
- Free

BRIGHTON BEACH ✪

77D2
Brighton Beach
Good

The decline of residential Brighton Beach more or less matched that of nearby Coney Island until the mid-1970s, when one of the unexpected results of the easing of immigration restrictions of Soviet Jewry was the arrival in the area of the first of what would become some 20,000 immigrants from the former Soviet Union. The initial slow influx became a flood through the 1980s and, following the collapse of the Soviet Union, still more arrived to join family members settled here. Cyrillic signs advertising caviar and vodka and scores of lively Russian restaurants are the main indications that this is the largest Russian community in the US.

CONEY ISLAND ✪

76C2
Surf Avenue between W 37th Street and Ocean Parkway
718/372 0275
Stillwell Avenue–Coney Island Good
Museum moderate, Astroland expensive

Up until the 1940s, Coney Island not only promised New Yorkers a day by the sea for the price of a subway ride, but provided the additional allure of state-of-the-art fairground rides and assorted lowbrow theatrical events, from peepshows to freakshows. Up to a million people a day flocked here to be seduced by the rollercoasters and rifle ranges, or simply to stroll the coastal Boardwalk munching a hotdog from the celebrated Nathan's Famous (a fast-food outlet said to be the originator of the hotdog).

After decades of neglect, Coney Island has enjoyed a revitalisation and been recognised as a living piece of Americana. Diverse exhibits from its glory days are displayed at the Coney Island Museum, which also organises local walking tours. Near by, the towering Cyclone roller coaster continues to provide gravity-defying rides and forms part of the thrills and spills offered at the Astroland Amusement Park. More sedate ways to pass the time include the greatly expanded New York Aquarium, featuring a re-created rocky coastal habitat complete with walruses, seals, penguins and sea otters.

The wooden Wonder Wheel, one of the classic fairground rides from the halcyon days of Coney Island

Queens

With 2 million people spread across 119 square miles, Queens is in part all-American suburbia, but also holds an ethnic mix of long-established Italians and Greeks alongside more recently arrived Koreans, Indians, Chinese and Japanese. The neighbourhood has a complex street numbering system that tends to confuse locals as often as visitors, though its places of particular interest are relatively easy to find.

A typically suburban street in Queens

The single area best representing Queens past and present is Flushing, which holds a large Asian population yet retains the Friends Meeting House (136–16 Main Street) and the nearby Bowne House that both date from the 17th century. In 1939, New York demonstrated its recovery from the Depression with a World's Fair in Flushing Meadows-Corona Park (immediately east of Flushing), its success prompting a second fair in 1964. Among the surviving items are Philip Johnson's New York State Pavilion Building and the 140-foot-high Unisphere, depicting the earth and her satellites.

Lining the East River, Astoria is one of the world's largest Greek communities and claims countless Greek bakeries, cafés and restaurants. Curiously, in the days before the industry shifted to Hollywood, the nascent US film industry was based in New York, and in 1919 the company that evolved into Paramount Pictures opened a studio in Astoria. The American Museum of the Moving Image now stands on the studio's site (junction of 35th Avenue and 36th Street). The museum records the era with costumes, props, film-making equipment and vintage movie posters, and features many more general exhibits on film and television themes.

Staten Island

Totally unlike any other part of New York City, Staten Island is dominated by hills, trees and greenery. Its slow pace and pastoral appearance could be reasons enough to visit, but it also holds a sprinkling of enjoyable historical sites, an excellent collection of Tibetan religious art and sees regular open-air events throughout the summer.

The island is linked to Brooklyn by the imposing Verazzano-Narrows Bridge – which greatly increased the island's population following its completion in the 1960s – and to Manhattan by the Staten Island ferry. Though much romanticised, the ferry is actually no more than a large boat but the views of Manhattan on the return journey, the Statue of Liberty, and the island's commercial traffic, can be exceptional – and the journey is free.

The Staten Island ferry plies between the wooded hills of Staten Island and the skyscraper-covered southern tip of Manhattan. Aside from being a travel boon to island-dwelling Financial District workers, the ferry provides outstanding views of Manhattan

ALICE AUSTEN HOUSE ⭐⭐

Given a camera by her uncle in 1884, Alice Austen went on to take around 8,000 photographs that provide a remarkable documentary of turn-of-the-century American domestic life. Despite the quality of her photos, Austen remained unknown and only shortly before her death in 1952 did her photos find wide attention, following the publication of some of them in *Life* magazine. A short film describes Austen's life and some of her possessions and photos fill this attractive bayside home into which the Austen family moved in 1868.

✚ 76B2
✉ 2 Hylan Boulevard
☎ 718/816 4506
🕐 Thu–Sun 12–5; closed Jan and Feb
🚌 S51
♿ Few
💲 Moderate

CONFERENCE HOUSE ⭐

The stone-built Conference House, originally known as the Billopp House and raised for a British naval captain, dates from 1680. It earned its new name as the venue of the only attempt to broker a peace between the Americans and the English after the Declaration of Independence. Held in September 1776, the negotiations proved futile but provided an excuse to turn the building, which served for a time as a rat-poison factory, into a museum with period furnishings and an intriguing display on the failed talks.

✚ 76A1
✉ 7455 Hylan Boulevard
☎ 718/984 2086
🕐 Fri–Sun 1–4; closed Dec, Jan, Feb and Mar
🚌 S78
♿ Few
💲 Moderate

GARIBALDI MEUCCI MUSEUM ⭐

Later to become one of the founders of independent, unified Italy, Giuseppe Garibaldi lived on Staten Island for two years in the 1850s having been forced to flee his homeland. Employed as a candle-maker, Garibaldi lived in this house that then belonged to Italian-American inventor Antonio Meucci. Letters, personal items and other knick-knacks document Garibaldi's period of occupancy.

A companion exhibit describes Meucci's life and achievements, not least his inventing of the telephone – an idea he unfortunately failed to patent.

✚ 76B2
✉ 420 Tompkins Avenue
☎ 718/442 1608
🕐 Tue–Sun 1–5
🚌 S78
♿ Few
💲 Free

JACQUES MARCHAIS MUSEUM OF TIBETAN ART ⭐⭐

A Wheel of Life, incense burners, ritual objects and other items from the world's Buddhist cultures (all accompanied by informative explanatory text) are among the collection of curiosities gathered in this stone cottage designed to resemble part of a Tibetan mountain temple. The extraordinary stash began with the discovery of 12 Tibetan figurines in the family attic by the 12-year-old girl of the house, Jacqueline Norman Klauber, who later adopted the professional name of Jacques Marchais and expanded the collection until her death in 1947. This fascinating museum enjoys a lovely hillside setting; the Dalai Lama is just one visitor who left impressed.

✚ 76B2
✉ 338 Lighthouse Avenue
☎ 718/987 3500
🕐 Apr–Nov Wed–Sun 1–5; Dec–Mar Wed–Fri 1–5
🚌 S74
♿ Few
💲 Moderate

76B2
441 Clarke Avenue
718/351 1611
Sep–Jun Wed–Fri 1–5;
Jul–Aug Wed–Fri 10–5,
Sat–Sun 1–5
S74
Few
Moderate

RICHMOND TOWN HISTORIC VILLAGE ✪✪

The fruits of 50 years of gathering and restoring 17th- to 19th-century buildings on a 100-acre site, the Richmond Town Village provides a telling peek into bygone days. Period-attired local history enthusiasts lead visitors around the buildings, often furnished with their original occupants' possessions, describing the trials and tribulations of Staten Island life in times past. During summer, the craft workshops are staffed by blacksmiths, shoemakers and carpenters demonstrating the old skills.

The oldest of the many noteworthy buildings is the 1695 Voorlezer's House, a church, school and home for the lay minister of the Dutch Reform Church. The far grander Greek Revival Third County Courthouse dates from 1837 and functions as a visitor centre. Across Center Street, the Historical Museum provides an absorbing overview of the island's changing fortunes and the industries, from brewing to oyster harvesting, that have underpinned its often fragile economy.

The Old Chapel that forms part of the leafy Snug Harbor Cultural Center dates from 1856

76B3
1,000 Richmond Terrace
718/448 2500
Dawn–dusk
S40
Good
Free

SNUG HARBOR CULTURAL CENTER ✪✪

While its tree-lined lanes would be enjoyable to stroll in any circumstances, the 83 acres of Snug Harbor Cultural Center are also dotted with preserved 19th-century buildings. Several of them serve a cultural function: the Newhouse Gallery displays works by living American artists in changing exhibitions; and the Veteran's Hall is a venue of concerts and recitals. In summer, the South Meadow stages outdoor concerts while the attractive Sculpture Park is filled with interesting works. The Botanic Garden and a small Children's Museum provide more reason to linger in an area originally known as Sailor's Snug Harbor, created to provide homes for 'decrepit and worn out sailors'.

Where To...

Above: *the Chelsea Hotel*

Restaurants

Prices
£ = up to $15
££ = $15–40
£££ = above $40

Except for the most expensive of the city's restaurants, where dinner will easily cost upwards of $60, excluding wine, for two people (lunch will be less; typically around $40), New York dining is a generally cost effective experience. Anticipate spending $7–$9 per person for breakfast, $9–$15 for lunch and $15–$30 for dinner excluding drinks and tip. Wherever you dine, a tip of at least 15 per cent of the total is expected; reward good service with a tip of 20 per cent or more.

Chelsea

Bottino (££–£££)
Among the trendiest eateries in the increasingly trendy Chelsea, offering mostly Tuscan-influenced fare and especially strong on seafood.
☒ 246 Tenth Avenue ☎ 212/206 6766 ☼ Lunch and dinner ☺ 23rd Street

Cafe Taj (£)
Small and friendly Indian eaterie with a small, good quality menu; everything is well-priced and the set meals offer exceptional value.
☒ 336 Eighth Avenue ☎ 212/807 6673 ☼ Lunch and dinner ☺ 23rd Street

Chelsea Grill (£–££)
Neighbourhood favourite that offers quality diner food in a comfortable setting; the burgers in particular have many admirers.
☒ 135 Eighth Avenue ☎ 212/242 5336 ☼ Lunch and dinner ☺ 14th Street–Eighth Avenue

Eighteenth and Eighth (£–££)
American and Caribbean fare, but mostly visited for the low prices, large portions and the often gregarious atmosphere, best sampled at the weekend brunch.
☒ 159 Eighth Avenue ☎ 212/242 5000 ☼ Breakfast, lunch and dinner ☺ 18th Street

Empire (£–££)
This dependable round-the-clock diner has become a neighbourhood institution offering omelettes, burgers, sandwiches, and lots more, to an exotic clientele of gallery-goers, nightclubbers, fashion models, as well as the simply peckish.
☒ Tenth Avenue at 22nd Street ☎ 212/243 2736 ☼ Open 24 hours ☺ 23rd Street

Royal Siam (££)
Popular spot for a good range of Thai favourites, and a promising selection of vegetarian main courses.
☒ 240 Eighth Avenue ☎ 212/741 1732 ☼ Lunch and dinner ☺ 23rd Street

Chinatown

Bo Ky (£)
Unpretentious noodle shop with tasty soups at unbeatable prices.
☒ 80 Bayward Street ☎ 212/406 2292 ☼ Breakfast, lunch and dinner ☺ Canal Street

Golden Unicorn (££)
A favourite for large family banquets or big parties. Large selection of dishes from savoury appetisers through dim sum to duck, fresh fish and bean curd.
☒ 18 East Broadway ☎ 212/941 0911 ☼ Breakfast, lunch and dinner ☺ Canal Street

HSF (£)
One of the better of the numerous Chinatown stops for lunchtime dim sum.
☒ 46 Bowery ☎ 212/374 1319 ☼ Breakfast, lunch and dinner ☺ Canal Street

Joe's Shanghai (£)
Range of Shanghai dishes but best known for its steamed buns, a selection of which make an inexpensive snack or a fuller meal, eaten from shared tables.
☒ 9 Pell Street ☎ 212/233 8888 ☼ Lunch and dinner ☺ Canal Street

Mandarin Court (£)
A lively spot for lunchtime dim sum; be prepared to shout your order.

📧 61 Mott Street 📞 212/608 3838 🍴 Lunch and dinner 🚇 Canal Street

New York Noodle Town (£)
Noodles in innumerable forms and with an immense choice of meat, seafood and vegetables to accompany them.
📧 28 Bowery 📞 212/349 0923 🍴 Breakfast, lunch and dinner 🚇 Grand Street

Sweet-n-Tart (£)
This hugely popular restaurant is noted for its dim sum but also serves a general range of Chinese dishes and delicious desserts.
📧 20 Mott Street 📞 212/964 0380 🍴 Breakfast, lunch and dinner 🚇 Canal Street

Viet-Nam (£)
Hole-in-the-wall Vietnamese eatery with a great-value menu.
📧 11 Doyers Street 📞 212/693 0725 🍴 Lunch and dinner 🚇 Canal Street

Wong Kee (£)
Cantonese cuisine at prices to please even the most budget-minded diner.
📧 113 Mott Street 📞 212/226 9018 🍴 Lunch and dinner 🚇 Canal Street

East Village and Lower East Side

Acme Bar and Grill (££)
Meat and fish dishes given a spicy Cajun treatment and smothered in fiery sauces.
📧 9 Great Jones Street 📞 212/420 1934 🍴 Lunch and dinner 🚇 Bleecker Street

Emerald Planet (£)
Inventively filled, healthy burritos.

📧 2 Great Jones Street 📞 212/353 9727 🍴 Lunch and dinner 🚇 Bleecker Street

Great Jones Café (££)
Red beans and rice, burgers, sandwiches plus other staples served to the accompaniment of a pulsating jukebox.
📧 54 Great Jones Street 📞 212/353 9727 🍴 Dinner only 🚇 Bleecker Street

Jules (££)
Modelled on a French bistro and serving simple but satisfying French-influenced fare in an informal setting, enlivened by live jazz each evening.
📧 65 St Mark's Place 📞 212/477 5560 🍴 Lunch and dinner 🚇 Astor Place

Mitali East (££)
Among the best of Manhattan's recent crop of Indian restaurants; also at 296 Bleecker Street (📞 212/989 1367).
📧 334 E 6th Street 📞 212/533 2508 🍴 Lunch and dinner 🚇 Astor Place

St Dymphna's Bar and Restaurant (£–££)
Plain and simple decor conceals some of the city's best modern Irish cuisine at a tempting price; a brick-walled patio offers a (sometimes) sunny spot to sample it.
📧 118 St Marks Place 📞 212/254 6636 🍴 Lunch and dinner 🚇 Astor Place

Yaffa Café (£)
Simple, mostly vegetarian fare.
📧 97 St Mark's Place 📞 212/674 9302 🍴 Always open 🚇 Astor Place

Dining with Children
In general, all but the most exclusive and expensive New York restaurants welcome children. Young diners will often be handed toys and colouring sets as soon as they sit down and those who are old enough to read will find they have their own section of the menu, where child-sized portions and perennial kids' favourites such as burgers, French fries and ice cream are strongly featured.

Street Eating

Few cities offer diners as much culinary choice as New York even before they set foot inside a restaurant. Throughout the city, street vendors can be found selling hot dogs, roasted chestnuts, pretzels, bagels and knishes (thin pastries filled with cheese, meat or potato). More sophisticated street stands might offer bowls of steaming noodles or falafel.

Financial District, Little Italy, SoHo and TriBeCa

Bennie's Thai Cafe (£)
Very affordable, very delicious Thai fare in a relaxed setting; deservedly packed at lunchtimes with local office workers but open daily until 9.
⊠ 88 Fulton Street ☎ 212/587 8930 ⊙ Lunch and dinner 🚇 Fulton Street

Chanterelle (£££)
An elegant setting for an elegant meal, make a reservation well in advance for one of New York's longest-established upscale eateries, where even the cheese choice is the stuff of gourmets' dreams.
⊠ 2 Harrison Street ☎ 212/966 6960 ⊙ Dinner 🚇 Franklin Street

Duane Park Café (£££)
Stylish bistro with an innovative use of Asian and American culinary ideas.
⊠ 157 Duane Street ☎ 212/732 5555 ⊙ Lunch and dinner; dinner only on Sat and Sun 🚇 Chambers Street

Franklin Station (££)
Popular locals' haunt with a mixture of French and Southeast Asian cooking.
⊠ 222 West Broadway ☎ 212/274 8525 ⊙ Lunch and dinner 🚇 Franklin Street

Mexican Radio (£)
Great value Mexican food served with a selection of fiery sauces in a tiny eatery that makes a great hideaway when exploring Little Italy and SoHo.
⊠ 19 Cleveland Place ☎ 212/343 0140 ⊙ Lunch and dinner 🚇 Spring St–Lafayette Street

Omen (£££)
A relaxed atmosphere as diners sample carefully prepared Japanese dishes.
⊠ 113 Thompson Street ☎ 212/925 8923 ⊙ Dinner 🚇 Spring Street

Raoul's (£££)
SoHo eatery masquerading as a French bistro, with a great choice of excellently prepared dishes.
⊠ 180 Prince Street ☎ 212/966 3518 ⊙ Dinner 🚇 Spring Street

Salaam Bombay (££)
A cut above most New York Indian eateries with a stylish ambience and extensive menu; the lunch buffet is pricey but good value.
⊠ 319 Greenwich Street ☎ 212/226 9400 ⊙ Lunch and dinner 🚇 Chambers Street

Toons (£–££)
The lunchtime buffet is the most cost-effective way to sample this highly-regarded quality Thai restaurant.
⊠ 363 Greenwich Street ☎ 212/925 7440 ⊙ Lunch and dinner 🚇 Franklin Street

Zoe (£££)
A bright, attractive SoHo loft setting and an inspired, eclectic menu helps make this one of the city's favourite restaurants for New Yorkers in the know.
⊠ 90 Prince Street ☎ 212/966 6722 ⊙ Lunch and dinner 🚇 Spring Street–Broadway

Greenwich Village

Anglers and Writers (££)
Cosy, welcoming niche for light fare; more substantial dishes also available.
⊠ 420 Hudson Street ☎ 212/675 0810 ⊙ Breakfast, lunch and dinner 🚇 Houston Street

Caffè Reggio (£)
Dark and atmospheric, this coffee house has been popular since 1927.
⊠ 119 Macdougal Street ☎ 212/475 9557 ⊙ Daily 🚇 W 4th Street

Cent'Anni (££)

Modest surroundings disguise what locals know to be a place of magical Florentine cuisine, with flavourful sauces, angel-hair pasta and carefully cooked meat.

🖂 50 Carmine Street
☎ 212/989 9494

Chumley's (££)

A prohibition-era speakeasy not only makes a great setting for an evening drink but also boasts classy versions of fish and chips, shepherds pie, and other bar favourites.

🖂 86 Bedford Street ☎ 212/675 4449 ⏰ Dinner; brunch Sat and Sun in winter 🚇 Sheridan Square–Christopher Street

Cornelia Street Cafe (££)

The downstairs jazz and poetry add a Greenwich Village mood to lunch or dinner drawn from an eclectic menu; also has a popular weekend brunch.

🖂 29 Cornelia Street ☎ 212/989 9319 ⏰ Lunch and dinner 🚇 W 4th Street–Washington Square

Corner Bistro (£)

Unpretentious locals' hangout where burger devotees will find their dreams come true.

🖂 331 West Fourth Street ☎ 212/242 9502 ⏰ Daily 🚇 Christopher Street

Cowgirl Hall of Fame (££)

Plaid-shirted staff ferry lashings of Tex-Mex fare and powerful margaritas to diners seated beneath photos of legendary cowgirls.

🖂 519 Hudson Street ☎ 212/633 1133 ⏰ Lunch and dinner 🚇 Houston Street

Cucina Stagionale (£)

Simple, inexpensive and very pleasing Italian food; be prepared to wait in the queue and to bring your own alcohol.

🖂 264 Bleecker Street ☎ 212/924 2707 ⏰ Lunch and dinner 🚇 Christopher Street

Elephant and Castle (£–££)

Wide-ranging and very affordable food, from substantial omelettes to imaginative sandwiches.

🖂 68 Greenwich Avenue ☎ 212/243 1400 ⏰ Breakfast, lunch and dinner 🚇 Christopher Street

Fish (£–££)

As the name suggests, serves produce of the sea in many forms with a varying but always fresh selection; the lunch specials can be exceptional value.

🖂 280 Bleecker Street ☎ 212/727 2879 ⏰ Lunch and dinner 🚇 Sheridan Square–Christopher Street

Le Gigot (£–££)

In the style of a French bistro, this compact and atmospheric spot offers a diverse and dependable menu, and serves a weekend brunch.

🖂 18 Cornelia Street ☎ 212/627 3737 ⏰ Lunch and dinner; closed Mon 🚇 W 4th Street–Washington Square

Gotham Bar and Grill (£££)

Make a reservation as early as possible for dinner at this long-trendy shrine to excellent eating; the fixed-price lunch is great value.

🖂 12 E 12th Street ☎ 212/620 4020 ⏰ Lunch and dinner 🚇 14th Street–Union Square

Home (£–££)

On a sunny day, the garden makes a welcome setting for sampling the innovative takes on traditional American fare, such as spicy pork chops, chicken and dumpling stew, grilled trout.

🖂 20 Cornelia Street ☎ 212/243 9579 ⏰ Lunch and dinner 🚇 W 4th Street–Washington Square

The Deli

Rare is the New York street corner that does not hold at least one deli. These offer all manner of sandwiches and rolls available with virtually any combination of toppings or fillings. Most delis also have a self-service area laden with fresh pasta, meats, vegetables and salad items paid for at the counter by weight.

Guided Eating

One of the best ways to discover the culinary thrills of Greenwich Village is with the three-hour walking and snacking tour run by Foods of New York Excursions (☎ 212/334 5070; www.foodsofny.com). These take in neighbourhood food shops and the insides of selected restaurants while describing local history. Price includes drinking water, a napkin, a map, and numerous snacks ranging from pizza slices to chocolate.

Hudson Corner Café (£)

Attractive diner serving some interesting pasta dishes alongside more common – but good quality – American fare.

✉ 570 Hudson Street ☎ 212/229 2727 🍴 Breakfast, lunch and dinner 🚇 Christopher Street

Japonica (££)

Spartan setting for substantial helpings of Japanese fare.

✉ 100 University Place ☎ 212/243 7752 🍴 Lunch and dinner 🚇 14th Street–Union Square

Little Havana (£–££)

Cuban food is making an impact in New York and this is one of the most enjoyable places to sample it; fare includes black bean soup, roasted salmon and vegetarian alternatives to traditionally meat-based dishes.

✉ 30 Cornelia Street ☎ 212/255 2212 🍴 Dinner 🚇 W 4th Street–Washington Square

Mama Buddha (£)

Meat, seafood and lots of vegetarian options comprise a tempting menu of well served Chinese dishes.

✉ 578 Hudson Street ☎ 212/924 2762 🍴 Lunch and dinner 🚇 Christopher Street

Minetta Tavern (££)

Long-serving Italian eatery serving dependable food in a pleasant old Greenwich Village atmosphere.

✉ 113 Macdougal Street ☎ 212/475 3850 🍴 Lunch and dinner 🚇 W 4th Street

Moustache (£–££)

Spinach pie, lamb sausages and falafel are among the offerings at this small and often busy Middle Eastern eatery.

✉ 90 Bedford Street ☎ 212/229 2220 🍴 Lunch and dinner 🚇 Sheridan Square–Christopher Street

One If By Land, Two If By Sea (£££)

This converted 19th-century carriage house makes a fine setting for a romantic candlelit dinner.

✉ 17 Barrow Street ☎ 212/228 0822 🍴 Dinner 🚇 Christopher Street

Pesce Pasta (£–££)

Highly regarded by locals for its tasty northern and southern Italian fare; the menu includes a fine range of seafood.

✉ 262 Bleecker Street ☎ 212/645 2993 🍴 Lunch and dinner 🚇 Sheridan Square–Christopher Street

Pink Teacup (££)

The deep southern American breakfasts featuring grits, bacon and sausages are popular; also Soulfood dishes such as black-eyed peas and collard greens.

✉ 42 Grove Street ☎ 212/807 6755 🍴 Breakfast, lunch and dinner 🚇 Christopher Street

Risotteria (£–££)

The risotto fanatic need look no further: the dish is served here in 40 different forms with a choice of three rice types.

✉ 270 Bleecker Street ☎ 212/924 6664 🍴 Lunch and dinner 🚇 Sheridan Square–Christopher Street

Silver Spurs (£)

Always busy coffee shop specialising in inventive omelettes and substantial burgers, plus only slightly less substantial vegeburgers.

✉ 771 Broadway ☎ 212/473 5517 🍴 Breakfast, lunch and dinner 🚇 8th Street–NYU

Suzie's (£)

Exceptional value in a long list of noodle and rice dishes, plus some inviting specials.

✉ 163 Bleecker Street ☎ 212/777 1395 🍴 Lunch and dinner 🚇 W 4th Street

Tea and Sympathy (£)

Comfort food for homesick Brits – as well as the traditional high tea, they also serve shepherd's pie, fish cakes and stodgy puddings.

✉ 108 Greenwich Avenue ☎ 212/807 8329 🕐 Lunch and dinner 🚇 14th Street

Tio Pepe (£–££)

Overwhelming décor but with good Spanish and Mexican dishes.

✉ 168 W 4th Street ☎ 212/ 242 9338 🕐 Lunch and dinner 🚇 W 4th Street

University Place (£)

Often crowded coffee shop which provides the usual diner fare at low prices. Excellent waffles, covered by ice-cream or strawberries.

✉ University Place and 12th Street ☎ 212/475 7727 🕐 Breakfast, lunch and dinner 🚇 14th Street–Union Square

White Horse Tavern (£–££)

Standard sandwiches, burgers and other dishes at the watering hole where Welsh poet Dylan Thomas drank his last in the 1950s.

✉ 567 Hudson Street ☎ 212/ 243 9260 🕐 Lunch and dinner 🚇 Christopher Street

Midtown Manhattan

Cabana Carioca (££)

Major portions of Brazilian food and a vibrant mood.

✉ 123 W 45th Street ☎ 212/581 8088 🕐 Lunch and dinner 🚇 Times Square

Cafe Edison (£–££)

Off the lobby of the art deco Edison Hotel, this busy diner has a full-range of diner staples for breakfast, lunch and dinner, with a few Jewish and Polish specialities also on the menu.

✉ 228 W 47th Street ☎ 212/354 0368 🕐 Breakfast, lunch and dinner 🚇 Times Square–42nd Street

Café Un Deux Trois (£££)

The French bistro fare served here speedily is ideal for most theatre-goers.

✉ 123 W 44th Street ☎ 212/354 4148 🕐 Lunch and dinner 🚇 Times Square

Chevys Fresh Mex (££)

Part of a nationwide chain but a fun place for the family discovering Mexican food, with a big list range of fajitas, tortillas and much more.

✉ 259 W 42nd Street ☎ 212/302 4010 🕐 Lunch and dinner 🚇 Times Square–42nd Street

Dean and Deluca Cafe (£–££)

A New York institution for their gourmet snacks, Dean and Deluca's quality nibbles and hot drinks make a welcome find in this tourist area.

✉ 235 W 46th Street ☎ 212/869 6890 🕐 Breakfast, lunch and dinner; closes 8PM Sun and Mon 🚇 42nd Street

Delegates' Dining Room (££)

Armed with a reservation and proper attire, the public can rub shoulders with United Nations officials and delegates (those who eat here are unlikely to be famous faces) on any weekday lunchtime. Top value is the buffet.

✉ United Nations, First Avenue at 46th Street ☎ 212/963 7626 🕐 Lunch only Mon–Fri. Reservations. ID required

Ellen's Stardust Diner (£–££)

Retro-diner packed with '1950s' memorabilia and staff regularly bursting into song; the menu offers classic diner fare such as meatloaf, waffles, burgers and milkshakes but the theatrical staff and setting are the draw.

✉ 1650 Broadway (at 51st Street) ☎ 212/956 5151 🕐 Breakfast, lunch and dinner 🚇 50th Street–Broadway

The Four Seasons

Many of New York's critic-pleasing restaurants serve outstanding food but only at the Four Seasons is the architecture as big a talking point as the food. The restaurant lies inside the Seagram Building, Mies Van Der Rohe's International Style masterpiece, and was designed by Philip Johnson. From the lighting to the napkins, every last detail of the walnut-panelled dining room has been thoughtfully planned and expertly crafted.

Mealtimes

Most coffee shops open for breakfast around 6AM and are generally at their busiest around 8AM. Some New Yorkers take lunch as early as 11:30AM but most dine between noon and 2PM. Dinner usually begins around 5PM and continues to around 9PM, although many establishments are open later and specialise in serving late meals to customers fresh from theatre-going. Dining hours are very flexible, however, and in the city that never sleeps numerous eateries stay open around the clock.

Firebird Cafe (££)

Trade the New York street scene for a peek into pre-Revolutionary Russia with grilled sturgeon and chicken tabaka among the main courses served in a palace-like setting; the truly decadent might start with champagne and caviar.

📧 363 W 46th Street ☎ 212/586 0244 🍽 Lunch and dinner; closed Mon 🚇 50th Street

Four Seasons (£££)

Inside the landmark Seagram Building and consistently rated as one of the best up-market dining experiences in New York.

📧 99 E 52nd Street ☎ 212/754 9494 🍽 Lunch and dinner 🚇 Lexington–Third Avenue

Harley Davidson Café (£–££)

Few genuine bikers would eat at this theme restaurant devoted to the legendary motorcycle manufacturer; serves American staples such as burgers, chicken wings and sandwiches.

📧 56th Street at Sixth Avenue ☎ 212/245 6000 🍽 Lunch and dinner 🚇 Times Square

John's Pizzeria (££)

John's thin crusts defined New York pizza from their original Greenwich Village base; whole pizzas or slices from this Midtown branch should match any in the city.

📧 260 W 44th Street ☎ 212/391 7560 🍽 Lunch and dinner; closes 9PM Sun 🚇 42nd Street

Lipstick Café (££)

Delectable breakfasts and lunches served to a fast-moving hungry office crowd.

📧 885 Third Avenue ☎ 212/486 8664 🍽 Breakfast and lunch; closed Sat and Sun 🚇 Lexington–Third Avenue

Mars 2112 (££)

Among the most imaginative of the city's many theme restaurants, here diners mingle with extra-terrestrials while sampling 'inter-galactic fusion cuisine' that bears a surprising similarity to upscale American diner fare.

📧 Corner of 51st and Broadway ☎ 212/582 2112 🍽 Lunch and dinner 🚇 50th Street–Broadway

Nirvana (£££)

Top of the range Indian food is the culinary attraction, but most people come for the fabulous view: a panorama of Central Park from 15-storeys high in a dining room disguised as a tent.

📧 30 Central Park S ☎ 212/658 6500 🍽 Lunch and dinner 🚇 59th Street–Fifth Avenue

Planet Hollywood (£–££)

Celebrity-owned worldwide chain that is always busy and probably the most enjoyable of New York's many theme restaurants.

📧 140 W 57th Street ☎ 212/333 7872 🍽 Lunch and dinner 🚇 57th Street

The Sea Grill (£££)

Cool blue decor creates a suitably ocean-like setting for the creations of one of the city's finest seafood chefs; choose from Chilean sea bass, crab cakes, mahi-mahi and lots more, inventively cooked and stylishly presented.

📧 Rockefeller Plaza, 19W 49th Street ☎ 212/332 7610 🍽 Lunch and dinner; closed Sun, dinner only Sat 🚇 49th Street

Victor's Café 52 (££)
Plantains, black beans, rice and other staples of Cuban cuisine, served with meat or fish in a lively setting.
✉ 236 W 52nd Street
☎ 212/586 7714 🕐 Lunch and dinner 🚇 Seventh Avenue

Zen Palate (£)
Ultra-healthy vegetarian food presented in delicately arranged portions.
✉ 34 Union Square East
☎ 212/614 9291 🕐 Lunch and dinner 🚇 14th Street–Union Square

Upper East Side
Brother Jimmy's (£)
Sometimes rowdy spot for substantial sandwiches, soups, barbecued ribs and other accompaniments to beer drinking and watching sports TV.
✉ 1644 Third Avenue
☎ 212/426 2020 🕐 Lunch and dinner 🚇 96th Street

Ciao Bella Gelato Cafe (£)
A hole-in-the-wall provider of sorbets, frozen yoghurts and ice cream in myriad flavours, certain to cool and calm the most demanding customer.
✉ 27 E 92nd Street ☎ 212/831 5555 🕐 All day 🚇 96th Street

Daniel (£££)
Immensely popular for high-quality French cuisine from one of the city's leading chefs.
✉ 60 E 65th Street ☎ 212/288 0033 🕐 Lunch and dinner 🚇 68th Street

Maya (££)
Delicious and flavourful upmarket Mexican main courses and inspired desserts; the margaritas are smooth and potent.

✉ 1191 First Avenue ☎ 212/585 1818 🕐 Lunch and dinner 🚇 63rd Street

Upper West Side
Barney Greengrass (££)
Long-running Jewish deli with all the usual favourites, but best known for its delicious sturgeon and salmon.
✉ 541 Amsterdam Avenue
☎ 212/724 4707 🕐 Breakfast and lunch 🚇 86th Street

Café Luxembourg (££–£££)
Lastingly popular French-style brassiere that draws knowledgeable diners to its eclectic, seasonally changing menu.
✉ 200 W 70th Street ☎ 212/873 7411 🕐 Lunch and dinner 🚇 72nd Street

EJ's Luncheonette (£)
Simple canteen setting for no-nonsense breakfasts, sandwiches, burgers and milkshakes. All reasoanably priced.
✉ 447 Amsterdam Avenue
☎ 212/873 3444 🕐 Breakfast, lunch and dinner 🚇 79th Street

Plum Tree (££–£££)
Vegetarian fare ranging from vegeburgers to creatively crafted pastas and stews.
✉ 1501 First Avenue ☎ 212/734 1412 🕐 Lunch and dinner; closed Mon 🚇 77th Street

Popover Café (£–££)
Pastry 'popovers' and a range of hearty soups, sandwiches and salads make this one of the neighbourhood's most popular stops for a filling snack.
✉ 551 Amsterdam Avenue
☎ 212/595 8555 🕐 Breakfast, lunch and dinner 🚇 86th Street

Brunch
A mix of late breakfast and early lunch, brunch is a popular Sunday event for many New Yorkers. Brunch usually lasts from 10AM to 2PM and typically costs $15 to $25, depending on the surroundings and the combination of food and drink included. The restaurant sections of local newspapers and magazines have plenty of brunch suggestions; reservations are strongly advised.

Accommodation

Prices and Taxes

The prices quoted by New York hotels very rarely include the cocktail of taxes added by the state and the city. These generally increase quoted rates by around 15 per cent. Before tax, the hotels listed on the following pages fall into the following low-season price categories (expect to pay 20 per cent more in hisgh season):

£ = under $100
££ = between $100 and $180
£££ = above $180

Amsterdam Court (££)

Friendly hotel with plush, well-priced rooms usefully located for the theatre district and for exploring Midtown Manhattan.
226 W 50th Street ☎ 212/459 1000; 1-800/341 9889 ⊜ 50th Street

Beacon (££)

Enterprising travellers will relish the rates and good-sized, well-equipped rooms at this Upper West Side hotel; a 24-hour coffee shop is on the premises.
2130 Broadway ☎ 212/787 1100; 1-800/572 4969 ⊜ 72nd Street

The Carlton (££)

Comfortable and elegantly furnished a few blocks from the hustle and bustle of Midtown Manhattan.
22 E 29th Street ☎ 212/532 4100; 1-800/542 1502 ⊜ 28th Street

Carlton Arms (£)

Each wacky, threadbare room is designed by a different (unknown) artist and what the Carlton Arms lacks in creature comforts (which is quite a lot) it just about makes up for through its sheer eccentricity. Expect bizarre fellow guests and exceptionally low prices.
25th Street at Third Avenue ☎ 212/679 0680 ⊜ 23rd Street

Carlyle (£££)

For many years a favourite of upper-crust visitors; the public rooms have crystal chandeliers, the private rooms have every amenity and the service is impeccable.
35 E 76th Street ☎ 212/744 1600; 1-800/227 5737 ⊜ 68th Street

Chelsea Savoy (££)

In the heart of the increasingly trendy Chelsea neighbourhood and making a comfortable base for exploring the highly-regarded restaurants and art galleries virtually on the doorstep, as well as being well-placed for the rest of Manhattan.
204 W 23rd Street ☎ 212/929 9535 ⊜ 23rd Street

Chelsea Star (£)

Small themed rooms with shared bathrooms and some of the lowest prices to be found on the edge of the fashionable Chelsea neighbourhood and in the shadow of the Empire State Building; even cheaper are the four-bed dormitories.
300W 30th Street ☎ 212/244 7827 ⊜ 34th Street–Penn Station

Comfort Inn Murray Hill (££)

This branch of the nationwide chain predictably has higher rates than its far-flung counterparts but nonetheless represents good value for New York City, with tidy, comfortable rooms.
35th Street between Fifth and Sixth avenues ☎ 800/228 5150 ⊜ 35th Street

Crowne Plaza at the United Nations (£££)

Nicely furnished and well-equipped rooms – perfect for a few relaxing nights.
304 E 42nd Street ☎ 212/986 8800; 1-800/879 8836 ⊜ Grand Central

Deauville (££)

Appealingly priced well-furnished rooms and just right for a relaxing stay; occupies a 19th-century brownstone house just off the busiest

Midtown thoroughfares.
📠 103 E 29th Street ☎ 212/683 0990; 1-800/333 8843
🚇 28th Street

Edison (£–££)

Not only an affordable choice for the Times Square area but also a delight for art deco fans, raised in 1931 the 700-room hotel has a friendly ambience despite its size.
📠 228 W 47th Street
☎ 212/840 5000 🚇 50th Street

Empire ££)

Trendsetting hotel offering small, well-furnished rooms all with CD, tape deck, colour TV and VCR. The grand lobby displays a beautiful collection of model stage sets – appropriate for a hotel just a few steps from the Lincoln Center on Broadway.
📠 Broadway at 63rd Street
☎ 212/265 7400; 1-888/822 3555
🚇 66th Street

Four Seasons (£££)

Among the tallest and most opulent of the New York hotels, each room cost an average of a million dollars to create and comes equipped, among other things, with a voluminous bathtub.
📠 57th Street between Park and Madison avenues
☎ 212/758 5700; 1-800/332 3442
🚇 59th Street

Gershwin (£–££)

The Campbell's soup can autographed by Andy Warhol that sits in the lobby is just the start for a highly individualistic property where every room has a Pop Art theme and handpainted murals.
📠 7 E 27th Street ☎ 212/545 8000 🚇 28th Street

Herald Square (£)

Occupying the 1893 *Life* magazine building, with mementoes of the publication easy to spot, the rooms are all spartan but with clean, tiled bathrooms. The main attraction is the cheap rate.
📠 31st Street near Fifth Avenue
☎ 1-800/727 1888; 212/279 4017

Hilton Times Square (££–£££)

In the pulsating heart of the Times Square district but with quiet and sumptuous furnished rooms; at the inviting cocktail bar, drinks are pricey but the wonderful views are free.
📠 234 W 42nd Street ☎ 212/840 8222 🚇 Times Square–42nd Street

Holiday Inn Downtown (££)

A rare hotel in Chinatown that makes the most of its limited space with well-appointed if modest rooms; some of the best-value Chinese restaurants are just outside the door.
📠 138 Lafayette Street
☎ 212/966 8898; 1-800/HOLIDAY
🚇 Lafayette Street

Howard Johnson–34th Street (££)

Branch of the nationwide chain that offers good value in a promising location just across from Madison Square Garden, a stone's throw from the Empire State Building and within walking distance of both Times Square and up-and-comimg Chelsea. A modest self-service breakfast is included.
📠 215 W 34th Street ☎ 212/947 5050; 1-800 633 1911 🚇 34th Street–Penn Station

Making Reservations

Most New York hotels can be booked online, either through their own sites or one of a multitude of online booking agencies (➤ 102) using a credit card. Booking online can bring savings although some discounted rates are only available if paid in full at the time of booking. A reservation made by phone or fax will usually be held until 6PM on the day of arrival but can be secured for the night with a deposit, usually made by quoting a valid credit card number.

Hotel Web Sites

www.beaconhotel.com
www.carltonhotel-ny.com
www.carltonarms.com
www.thecarlyle.com
www.chelseasavoynyc.com
www.starhotelny.com
www.comfortinn manhattan.com
www.unitednations. crowneplaza.com
www.edisonhotelnyc.com
www.fourseasons.com
www.gershwinhotel.com
www.heraldsquarehotel.com
www.hilton.com
www.sixcontinentshotels.com/holiday-inn
www.hojopennstation.com
www.hudsonnyc.com
www.larchmonthotel.citysearch.com
www.michelangelohotel.com
www.newyorkerhotel.com
www.rogersmithhotel.citysearch.com
www.nycsalisbury.com
www.wshotel.com
www.wolcott.com

Reservation Services

A plethora of online booking services offer competitive rates on New York hotels. Most are also contactable on toll-free phone numbers:
www.hotelusa.com;
www.hotels-in-new-york.com (☎ 1-800/295 0326);
www.180096hotel.com (Hotel Reservation Network; ☎ 1-800/364 0801); and
www.accommodationsexpress.com (☎ 1-800/277 1064). Reservations can also be made through www.newyork.citysearch.com.

Hudson (££)

Another Ian Schrager-owned, Philippe Starck-designed hotel setting the pace for fashionable boutique hotels. Although small, the rooms are torn from a design magazine's pages and the public areas are thronged by New York scene setters.

✉ 365W 58th Street ☎ 212/554 6000 🚇 59th Street

Larchmont (£–££)

Shared bathrooms help make the Larchmont an affordable base in the heart of Greenwich Village and for discovering the city without the hustle and bustle common to Midtown Manhattan.

✉ 27 W 11th Street ☎ 212/989 9333 🚇 Sixth Avenue

Michelangelo (£££)

18th- and 19th-century European art, marble and crystal help the Michelangelo rank among New York's most luxurious hotels.

✉ 51st Street at Seventh Avenue ☎ 212/765 1900; 1-800/947 5050 🚇 7th Avenue or Rockefeller Center

Morgans (£££)

Design-conscious lodgings from one of the creators of the legendary Studio 54 disco, Morgans draws a fashionable crowd and the staff pride themselves on expecting the unexpected.

✉ 237 Madison Avenue ☎ 212/ 686 0300; 1-800/334 3408 🚇 33rd Street

Murray Hill East Suites (£££)

Every room is a suite and has a well-appointed kitchenette making this a good choice for those travelling with a family or who simply crave space.

✉ 149 E 39th Street ☎ 212/661 2100; 1-800/248 9999 🚇 42nd Street–Grand Central

The Muse (££–£££)

Discover what feng shui can do for a good night's sleep in this minimalist-designed hotel where a palm meter measures the energy level of new arrivals so they can be assigned a room of suitable colour.

✉ 140 W 46th Street ☎ 877/692 6873 🚇 Times Square/42nd Street

The New Yorker (££)

Now part of the Radisson chain this impressively-restored 1930s art deco original has panoramic Manhattan views from many of its 800 rooms. Around the enormous lobby are several restaurants and a 24-hour coffee shop.

✉ 481 Eighth Avenue at 34th Street ☎ 212/971 0101; 1-800/764 4680 🚇 34th Street–Penn Station

Park Savoy (£)

Clean, comfortable rooms, the rates are remarkably low for a prime Midtown Manhattan location adjacent to Central Park.

✉ 158 W 58th Street ☎ 212/245 5755 🚇 Columbus Circle

Pioneer (£)

Very affordable, no-frills rooms in a SoHo location, the Pioneer is ideal for those on a tight budget and already acquainted with the city.

✉ 341 Broome Street ☎ 212/ 226 1482 🚇 Bowery

Plaza Athénée (£££)

The luxury begins at the plush lobby and continues to the ultra-comfortable rooms with European-style furnishings and with rose marble bathrooms; the costliest suites boast balconies with cinematic views.

✉ 37 E 64th Street ☎ 212/734 9100, 1-800/447 8800 🚇 Lexington Avenue

Roger Smith (£££)

Tastefully furnished rooms, attentive service and sensible rates are the appeal of this hotel in a promising Midtown Manhattan location.

⊠ 501 Lexington Avenue
☎ 212/755 1400; 1-800/445 0277
🚇 42nd Street–Grand Central

Royalton (£££)

Impressive Phillipe Starck-designed interior; clientele is young and image conscious.

⊠ 44th Street between Fifth and Sixth avenues ☎ 212/869 4400;
1-800/635 9013 🚇 42nd Street

Salisbury Hotel (£££)

Good-sized rooms with safes and refrigerators, plus many other good points.

⊠ 123 W 57th Street ☎ 212/246 1300; 1-888/NYC 5757 🚇 57th Street

SoHo Grand (£££)

One of the pioneering hotels to bring Midtown Manhattan comfort and service to the chic confines of SoHo in the 1990s, its bar and eatery still draw neighbourhood celebrities.

⊠ 310 W Broadway ☎ 212/965 3000, 1-800/965 3000 🚇 Canal Street

Tribeca Grand (£££)

Set around an eight-storey atrium and consuming an entire block, this hotel almost dwarfs the neighbourhood in which it sits. Atmosphere may be lacking but amenities are not, with luxurious furnishings, audio-visual entertainment centres, and free high-speed internet access in each room.

⊠ 2 Sixth Avenue ☎ 212/519 6600, 1-877/519 6600 🚇 Canal Street

Waldorf-Astoria (£££)

A sightseeing stop for its opulent lobby and place in New York history for the accommodating of royals and heads of state.

⊠ 301 Park Avenue ☎ 212/355 3000; 1-800/WALDORF 🚇 51st Street

Wales Hotel (££)

Long-serving hotel tucked away on the Upper East Side; includes a light breakfast and afternoon tea.

⊠ 1295 Madison Avenue
☎ 212/876 6000 🚇 96th Street

Washington Jefferson (£–££)

Few frills and the cheapest rooms have shared bathrooms, but attractively-priced for a Midtown Manhattan location a few blocks north of Times Square.

⊠ 318-328 W 51st Street
☎ 212/246 7550; 1-888/567 7550
🚇 50th Street–Eighth Avenue

Washington Square (££)

Some rooms are small, but excellent value in good location; breakfast included.

⊠ 103 Waverly Place
☎ 212/777 9515; 1-800/222 0418
🚇 W 4th Street

Wellington (££)

Except perhaps for the lobby, there is nothing fancy about the sizable Wellington. Rooms are clean, simple and very reasonably priced for their prized central location.

⊠ Seventh Avenue at 55th Street ☎ 212/247 3900; 1-800/652 1212 🚇 7th Avenue or 55th Street

Wolcott (£)

Modestly sized rooms at bargain rates in a Midtown Manhattan location.

⊠ 4 W 31st Street ☎ 212/268 2900 🚇 28th Street, 33rd Street or 34th Street

Wyndham (££)

Popular with Broadway performers. Good sized rooms at reasonable rates.

⊠ 58th Street ☎ 212/753 3500
🚇 Seventh Avenue or 55th Street

Credit Cards

Guests paying by credit card will have an imprint made of their card on arrival and will usually simply sign for the total amount owed when checking out. Guests not intending to pay by credit card must be prepared to pay in advance with cash or travellers' cheques.

Department Stores & Shopping Centres

Computers
Computers, computer accessories and software can be considerably less expensive in the US than elsewhere, although anyone buying hardware should check the different electrical requirements of the equipment they are buying (software, by contrast, will work on any compatible computer). One of the major outlets is CompUSA with branches across the city including 1775 Broadway, on the corner with 57th Street (☎ 1-800/COMPUSA).

Barney's
Opened to much fanfare in 1993, New York's largest new clothing outlet for years has international designer names, expensive restaurants and even a pricey gym so you can hone your body.
✉ 660 Madison Avenue
☎ 212/826 8900 🚇 60th Street

Bergdorf Goodman
When money is no object, New Yorkers come here to buy their clothes beneath crystal chandeliers and be fussed over by attentive, professional staff; a full range of accessories is also to hand. Bergdorf Men is directly across Fifth Avenue.
✉ 745 Fifth Avenue ☎ 212/753 7300 🚇 59th Street

Bloomingdale's
Pulsating with noise and colour, Bloomingdale's is New York-style consumerism at its far-from-demure best; be it ceramics, books, clothing or perfume, everything is hawked with a religious fervour and special promotions are frequent.
✉ 1000 Third Avenue
☎ 212/705 2000 🚇 59th Street

Bradlees
This huge emporium is packed with just about everything you can think of at knock-down prices; don't expect high quality, though.
✉ Union Square ☎ 212/673 5814 🚇 14th Street

Lord and Taylor
More modestly sized than most, this lovely, somewhat old-fashioned store is particularly good for shirts, sweaters, trousers and skirts. The Christmas windows, featuring animated figures, are a delight.
✉ 424 Fifth Avenue ☎ 212/391 3344 🚇 Grand Central

Macy's
With ten floors and half a million items for sale, Macy's claim to be the largest department store in the world is entirely believable. Shoppers can sift through kitchenware, cosmetics, clothing, footwear, stop for lunch and a haircut, and even buy a souvenir from the Metropolitan Museum of Art. Be warned, though – you'll need plenty of stamina.
✉ 151 W 34th Street ☎ 212/695 4400 🚇 34th Street

Manhattan Mall
Aptly named, the nearest thing in Manhattan to an all-American shopping mall with a large array of well-known, mid-range stores spanning fashion, household, gifts, electronics, food and more.
✉ Sixth Avenue and 33rd Street ☎ 212/465 0500 🚇 34th Street

Sak's Fifth Avenue
Top-notch clothing, linens and cosmetics for those who value quality and traditional good taste over the vagaries of fashion. Known (and rightly so) for its good service.
✉ 611 Fifth Avenue ☎ 212/753 4000 🚇 Fifth Avenue

Takashimaya
Expect to pay high prices for beautiful things at this elegant Japanese emporium which comes complete with an atrium and a traditional tearoom where jaded spirits can be revived and aching feet rested.
✉ 693 Fifth Avenue ☎ 212/350 0100 🚇 54th or 55th Street

Art & Antiques

A La Vieille Russie
Quality antiques many of them representing the handiwork of the finest craftsmen of Tsarist Russia.
✉ 781 Fifth Avenue ☎ 212/752 1727 🚇 59th Street

AC Project Room
This artist-run space has plenty to tempt from creators whose work has yet to command inflated prices.
✉ Second floor, 453 W 17th Street ☎ 212/645 4970 🚇 14th Street–Eighth Avenue

Annexe Antique Galleries
Each Saturday and Sunday finds vendors and would-be buyers converging on this open-air space where the stalls groan under the weight of artworks, rugs, furniture, jewellery and more.
✉ 107–111 W 25th Street ☎ 212/463 0200 🚇 23rd Street

Forty Fifty Sixty
The costume jewellery is overshadowed by a remarkable stash of dolls from several eras.
✉ Lower Gallery #103, the Showplace, 40 W 25th Street ☎ 212/463 0980 🚇 23rd Street

Guggenheim Museum Store
Quality goodies from expensive pieces of art to affordable souvenirs: all modern and tasteful.
✉ 575 Broadway ☎ 212/423 3875 🚇 Prince Street

Leo Castelli Gallery
A gallery renowned for bringing the work of abstract expressionist and pop art notables to a wider audience, and still offering their works to well-heeled collectors.
✉ 420 West Broadway ☎ 212/431 5160 🚇 Spring Street or Prince Street

Manhattan Art and Antiques Center
Over 100 stores are grouped here under one roof to provide hours of browsing delight for the committed art and antique seeker.
✉ 1050 Second Avenue ☎ 212/355 4400 🚇 59th Street

Margo Feiden
Well-established gallery with many quality drawings, but best known for Al Hirschfeld's wonderful theatrical caricatures. Worth a look even if the prices are beyond your budget.
✉ 699 Madison Avenue ☎ 212/677 5330 🚇 Lexington Avenue–59th Street

Paula Cooper Gallery
One of the originators of the Chelsea art gallery scene and now an acknowledged showplace for semi-established, mostly New York-based names.
✉ 534 W 21st Street ☎ 212/255 1105 🚇 23rd Street

Pace Gallery
Prestigious gallery for the heavyweights of modern and contemporary art; particularly noted for rising names.
✉ 32 E 57th Street ☎ 212/421 3292 🚇 59th Street

White Trash
Bargains may be thin on the ground but this is almost certainly the city's premier purveyor of lamps and other furnishings, plus some less costly bric-a-brac, all original or in the style of the 1950s.
✉ 304 E 5th Street ☎ 212/598 5956 🚇 Second Avenue

Chelsea Antiques Building
Antique seekers lacking the energy for a trawl around Manhattan's individual retailers might head instead for the Chelsea Antiques Building (✉ 110 W 25th Street ☎ 212/929 0909 🚇 23rd Street) where 150 dealers can be found across 12 floors. Items for sale include 18th- and 19th-century furnishings, textiles, paintings, lamps, toys, pottery, books and comics, and there is a cappuccino/espresso bar to revive jaded browsers.

Clothes & Accessories

Niketown

Even in shopping-crazed New York, few consumer experiences can compete with a visit to Niketown (⊠ 6 E 57th Street ☎ 212/891 6543 ⊕ 59th Street), a high-tech temple to the sportswear company spread across five floors with interactive CD-ROMs to assist customers in making their purchase. Among the choices to contend with are more than 1,000 types of footwear.

Banana Republic

Good middle-of-the-road duds for men and women at affordable prices.
⊠ 89 Fifth Avenue ☎ 212/366 4630 ⊕ Union Square

Betsey Johnson

Bold and colourful female fashions that fall just short of daring. Also at several other city locations.
⊠ 251 E 60th Street ☎ 212/319 7699 ⊕ 59th Street

Brooks Brothers

From overcoats to suits and shirts, conservative men's clothing rarely comes of a better quality than found here.
⊠ 346 Madison Avenue ☎ 212/682 8800 ⊕ Grand Central

Canal Jean Co

Brave the pulsating music and garish lighting for an exceptional horde of cut-rate jeans, sportswear, T-shirts, accessories and more.
⊠ 504 Broadway ☎ 212/226 1130 ⊕ Prince Street

Cartier

Gold, silverware and porcelain that is the stuff of dreams; prices reach the realms of the phantasmagorical.
⊠ 653 Fifth Avenue ☎ 212/753 0111 ⊕ 47th–50th Street

Daffy's

Bargains galore for those prepared to hunt through the rails looking for designer-label look-alikes. Also good for casual stuff.
⊠ 11 Fifth Avenue ☎ 212/529 4477 ⊕ Union Square

David Saity Jewelry

Rarely inexpensive but always unusual and intriguing Native American-made jewellery.
⊠ 450 Park Avenue ☎ 212/223 8125 ⊕ Lexington Avenue–59th Street

Ellen Christine Millery

Stock of quality vintage clothing that spans the decades; the gathering of women's hats alone make a visit worthwhile.
⊠ 255 W 18th Street ☎ 212/242 2457 ⊕ 18th Street

Family Jewels Vintage Clothing

Everything from 1920s evening gowns to 1960s miniskirts can be found among these racks of vintage clothing, along with a selection of hats, handbags and shoes.
⊠ 130 W 23rd Street ☎ 212/633 6020 ⊕ 23rd Street

Fur Furgery

A popular spot when the New York winter kicks in, offering fake furs in myriad styles.
⊠ 208 W 29th Street ☎ 212/244 7601 ⊕ 34th Street–Avenue of the Americas

Genesis

If Bloomingdale's fails to please, cross the street to this well-stocked emporium, best-known for its classic American leather jackets but also stocking shirts, waistcoats and trousers.
⊠ 718 Lexington Avenue ☎ 212/980 1514 ⊕ 59th Street–Lexington Avenue

Hermès

Top-dollar silk scarves, handbags, belts and a well-stocked equestrian section to prepare for those horse-riding weekends.
⊠ 691 Madison Avenue ☎ 212/751 3181 ⊕ 59th Street

INA

Imposing designer garments, shoes and accessories for the lady with a full social diary, at reduced prices.
🖂 21 Prince Street ☎ 212/333 9048 🚇 Prince Street

Michaels' – The Consignment Shop For Women

Many is the well-heeled Upper East Side lady who sifts through the designer names sold here at lower-than-retail prices.
🖂 1041 Madison Avenue
☎ 212/737 7273 🚇 77th Street

Moe Ginsberg

Mostly men's clothing and footwear over four floors and featuring a host of top international fashion names at competitive prices.
🖂 162 Fifth Avenue
☎ 212/242 3482 🚇 23rd Street

Morgane le Fay

A collection of women's separates, jackets and dresses, bordering on the theatrical, for those who favour strong, plain colours.
🖂 67 Wooster Street
☎ 212/219 7672 🚇 Prince Street

OMG

One of five New York branches boasting a gigantic stock of top-name jeans at compelling prices, plus casual wear and accessories.
🖂 546 Broadway ☎ 212/925 9513 🚇 Prince Street

Polo/Ralph Lauren

Top-notch tweeds, cotton shirts and everything else for the man about Manhattan.
🖂 888 Madison Avenue
☎ 212/434 8000
🚇 68th Street–Hunter College

The Shirt Store

Discerning shirt wearers can choose from a choice of eight collars and have their chosen design made to order.
🖂 51 E 44th Street ☎ 212/557 8040 🚇 42nd Street–Grand Central

Stella Dallas

Vintage clothing, much of it men's and women's items from the 1950s.
🖂 218 Thompson Street
☎ 212/674 0447 🚇 W 4th Street

Tiffany & Co

Legendary store with three floors of highly desirable crystals, gold and silverware, clocks and jewellery, all at prices to suit the rich.
🖂 727 Fifth Avenue
☎ 212/755 8000 🚇 59th Street

Today's Man

Good-value store for men's clothing to suit any occasion. Lots of choice and a sprinkling of top labels.
🖂 625 Sixth Avenue
☎ 212/924 0200 🚇 23rd Street

Weiss and Mahoney

Engrossing collection of military uniforms, combat fatigues, field jackets, parkas and other items of army, navy and air force clothing and accessories.
🖂 142 Fifth Avenue
☎ 212/675 1915
🚇 14th Street–Union Square

212 Jewelry

When that special piece of jewellery remains elusive, be it necklace, cufflink, earrings or pendant, have it made to order here; expect to pay for the privilege.
🖂 9 Christopher Street ☎ 212/243 5213 🚇 Christopher Street–Sheridan Square

Museum Shops

Many of New York's fine museums have equally fine retail outlets attached, selling everything from posters of recent exhibitions to, in the case of the Guggenheim (▶ 105), constructivist mobiles certain to enliven your living room.
The Museum of Modern Art has a particularly strong stock of art books.

Books, CDs & Records

Tower Records
For the biggest stocks of records and CDs in New York, plus an endless selection of videos and books, visit one of the four branches of Tower Records where the best-selling items are often offered at reduced rates. The locations are Trump Tower, 725 Fifth Avenue; junction of 66th Street and Broadway; and two neighbouring branches at the junction of 4th Street and Broadway. All branches share a toll-free telephone number: ☎ 1-800/ASK TOWER.

Barnes and Noble
This is one of several Manhattan branches of this colossally well-stocked general bookstore that also boasts regular author readings and an inviting café with a fine selection of refreshments. It is said to contain over 3 million volumes.
✉ 4 Astor Place ☎ 212/420 1322 🚇 Astor Place

Biography Bookshop
As the name suggests, this store is packed from floor to ceiling with nothing but biographies.
✉ 400 Bleecker Street ☎ 212/807 8655 🚇 Christopher Street

Cosmic Comics
The proof that New York has inspired innumerable comic strips is here, amid thousands of new and used comic books, plus a wide range of comic-related paraphernalia.
✉ 36 E 23rd Street ☎ 212/460 5322 🚇 23rd Street–Park Avenue

Forbidden Planet
Immense stocks of science-fiction and fantasy books and comics from the 1930s to the present day, plus sci-fi paraphernalia of all kinds to suit all tastes.
✉ 840 Broadway ☎ 212/473 1576 🚇 14th Street–Union Square

HMV Record Stores
Huge, general stock of CDs and records.
✉ 2081 Broadway at 72nd Street ☎ 212/721 5900 🚇 72nd Street

Partners and Crime
Crime and mystery specialists stocking new, classic and out-of-print titles, some at bargain prices, and also hosting readings and signings from prominent crime authors.
✉ 44 Greenwich Avenue ☎ 212/243 0440 🚇 Sheridan Square

A Photographer's Place
New and secondhand books about photo techniques and photographers.
✉ 133 Mercer Street ☎ 212/431 9358 🚇 Prince Street

Richard Stoddard Performing Arts Books
Out of print books and memorabilia, including programmes and autographs, relating to the performing arts.
✉ Room 937, 41 Union Square West ☎ 212/645 9576 🚇 Union Square

Rizzoli Bookstore
A cosy general bookstore with particularly good stocks of art and photography titles, including many discount bargains.
✉ 31 W 57th Street ☎ 212/759 2424 🚇 57th Street

Rocket Scientist Records
The perfect antidote to the chain stores, with new, used and imported records and CDs spanning otherwise hard-to-find rock, reggae, soul, jazz and Latin releases.
✉ 43 Carmine Street ☎ 212/242 0066 🚇 W Fourth Street

Strand Books
Cut-price new and secondhand books on all subjects arranged around 8 miles of shelving.
✉ 828 Broadway ☎ 212/463 1452 🚇 14th Street

Gifts, Oddities & Collectables

American Craftsman
One of several Manhattan branches stocking American-made chairs, lamps and ornaments.
✉ 317 Bleecker Street
☎ 212/727 0841 🚇 Christopher Street

Bruce Frank Beads and Ethnographic Art
Beads in more colours and shapes than you previously thought possible in materials ranging from bone to glass.
✉ 215 W 83rd Street ☎ 1/877 BEADS 75 🚇 86th Street

Colony Record and Music Center
Mainstream and obscure recordings from stage shows and other musical genres, plus posters, concert programs, and assorted memorabilia.
✉ 1619 Broadway ☎ 212/965 6009 🚇 Times Square–50th Street

Dragon Bazaar Inc
Just one of several souvenir stores along this Chinatown street, packed to the rafters with kites, porcelain figurines, painted chopsticks, tea services, Chinese horoscope paraphernalia, and much more at inviting prices.
✉ 2 Mott Street ☎ 212/732 6405 🚇 Canal Street

Enchanted Forest
Hand-crafted toys and children's books.
✉ 85 Mercer Street ☎ 212/925 6677 🚇 Prince Street

Green Flea Indoor/Outdoor Markets
Every Sunday, from 10AM, hundreds of stalls are laden with clothing, posters, leather goods, books, CDs and tapes, and much more, at unbeatable prices. Also on Saturday from 9AM at 67th Street between First and York avenues.
✉ Columbus Avenue at 77th Street ☎ 212/721 0900 🚇 79th Street

Maxilla and Mandible
Bones, fossils, mounted insects and seashells feature among a strange and captivating stock; cheaper are the posters of bats, wolves and spiders.
✉ 453 Columbus Avenue ☎ 212/724 6173 🚇 81st Street

Pleasure Chest
Erotic toys, dildos, love dolls, flavoured condoms and much more to enrich one's love life.
✉ 156 Seventh Avenue ☎ 212/242 2158 🚇 14th Street

SoHo Antiques Fair Collectibles and Crafts
Saturday and Sunday from 9AM finds all manner of collectibles – coins, books, rugs and ornaments to name a few – at inviting prices.
✉ Broadway and Grand Street ☎ 212/682 2000 🚇 Spring Street–Canal Street

Ten Rea Tea and Ginseng Co
The best place in New York to buy ginseng; also stocks a range of high-quality teas.
✉ 75 Mott Street ☎ 212/349 2286 🚇 Canal Street

World of Golf
The name says it all: packed with golf clubs, bags, balls, shirts, caps, books, videos, CDs, and even more things connected with golf.
✉ 147 E 47th Street ☎ 212/755 9398 🚇 51st Street; Lexington–Third Avenue

Manny's Music
Its walls lined by signed photos of celebrity customers and its floors covered in guitars, saxophones, pianos and everything else that can play a tune, Manny's Music (✉ 156 W 48th Street ☎ 212/819 0576 🚇 49th Street) is well worth a browse even for the hopelessly tone deaf. This self-styled museum of rock and roll has been in business for years and offers discount rates on the latest instruments and recording gear.

Children's Attractions

New York Skyride
Once the novelty of ascending to the observation levels of the Empire State Building (▶ 18) has worn off, visit the second floor's New York Skyride (☎ 1-888 SKYRIDE or 212/279 9777) where participants are given a virtual aerial tour of the city at dizzying speed aboard a 'spacecoptor'.

American Museum of Natural History
The dinosaur skeletons and the enormous blue whale are sure to turn young heads; the adjacent Hayden Planetarium, with its state-of-the-art astronomy exhibitions and guided tours of the night sky, is another favourite.
✉ Central Park West at 79th Street ☎ 212/769 5100 🚇 79th Street or 81st Street

Bronx Zoo
The largest zoo in the US (it claims to house over 4,000 animals) will easily keep youngsters of disparate ages amused for a full day, while the small furry inmates of the Children's Zoo will delight the infants (▶ 80).
✉ Bronx River Parkway, Fordham Road ☎ 718/367 1010 🚇 Pelham Parkway

Brooklyn Children's Museum
Entertaining tots since 1899 and claimed to be the world's longest serving children's museum; entertaining and educational exhibits by the score inside an architecturally innovative structure. Appealing to adults, too.
✉ 145 Brooklyn Avenue, Brooklyn ☎ 718/735 4400 🚇 Kingston Avenue

Central Park Carousel
One of the most kid-pleasing attractions in New York is also the simplest: this vintage carousel revolves amid the greenery of Central Park at impressive speed to a soundtrack of mechanically generated music.
✉ Central Park, just south of 65th Street Transverse 🚇 59th Street–Columbus Circle

Central Park Wildlife Conservation Center
Penguins, monkeys and bears are among the creatures inhabiting this 5.5-acre chunk of Central Park; children's activities include storytime each afternoon.
✉ 830 Fifth Avenue ☎ 212/861 6030 🚇 68th Street–Hunter College

Charles A Dana Discovery Center
On the northern edge of Central Park with engaging exhibits exploring environmental themes and special events such as birdwatching for beginners and an artist-led walk through the park describing and elucidating nature's inspirational qualities.
✉ 110th Street and Fifth Avenue ☎ 212/860 1370 🚇 110th Street

Chelsea Piers Lanes
Ten-pin bowling raised to fine art and with bumper bowling for younger kids. At night, 'extreme bowling' comes with music, fog machines, laser lights and Day-Glo pins.
✉ Between piers 59 and 60, west end of 23rd Street ☎ 212/835 2695 🚇 23rd Street

Children's Museum of the Arts
Here young people aged from 18 months to 10 years can enjoy a series of creative play areas based around the visual and performing arts.
✉ 182 Lafayette Street ☎ 212/941 9198 🚇 Spring Street

Children's Museum of Manhattan
State-of-the-art interactive exhibits explore the workings of the human body,

nature, and much else in this museum that fills several floors and provides endless opportunity for creative and entertaining play.

🖂 **The Tisch Building, 212 W 83rd Street** ☎ **212/721 1234** 🚇 **86th Street**

Enchanted Forest

A make-believe medieval forest inhabited by a galaxy of stuffed animals.

🖂 **85 Mercer Street** ☎ **212/925 6677** 🚇 **Spring Street**

FAO Schwarz

Possibly the world's most famous toyshop, packed from floor to ceiling with the kind of toys most children can only dream about.

🖂 **767 Fifth Avenue** ☎ **212/644 9400** 🚇 **Fifth Avenue**

Lazer Park

An inter-active adventure game through a 5000-square feet themed area with an obstacle at every turn, is just one of the games at this high-tech amusement centre; other delights include virtual reality simulations of tank driving and space exploration and assorted arcade games.

🖂 **1560 Broadway at 46th Street** ☎ **212/398 3060** 🚇 **42nd Street– Times Square**

Museum of the City of New York

The permanent collection of historic dolls' houses and vintage firefighting equipment may be enough for some children, but the museum also stages regular special events aimed specifically at kids (► 59).

🖂 **1220 Fifth Avenue and 103rd Street** ☎ **212/534 1672** 🚇 **103rd Street**

New York Transit Museum

On Wednesday and Saturday afternoons the museum holds child-aimed workshops to discover the marvels of city transport (► 85).

🖂 **130 Livingstone Street, Brooklyn** ☎ **718/330 3060** 🚇 **Boerum Place–Schemerhorn Street**

Sony Wonder Technology Lab

This outlet of the multinational corporation has regular programmes for children exploring the mysteries of animation and other media-related subjects with the aid of interactive computers and special weekend workshops.

🖂 **550 Madison Avenue** ☎ **212/833 8100** 🚇 **Fifth Avenue**

South Street Seaport Museum

Clambering around the historic ships here may well appeal to youngsters, although the museums less so. Throughout the summer months daily street entertainment is performed in the area.

🖂 **Fulton Street** ☎ **212/669 9400, 212/669 9420** 🚇 **Fulton Street**

Staten Island Children's Museum

While parents can explore the rest of Snug Harbor complex, those aged five to 12 can amuse themselves with the interactive exhibits and regular workshops. During the school holidays and at weekends, concerts are staged too.

🖂 **Snug Harbor Cultural Center, 1000 Richmond Terrace, Staten Island** ☎ **718/273 2060** 🚇 **S40**

Sightseeing with Kid Appeal

Central Park: (► 16)
Empire State Building: (► 18)
Forbes Magazine Galleries: (► 46)
Intrepid Sea-Air-Space Museum: (► 50)
National Museum of the American Indian: (► 60)
New York City Fire Museum: (► 61)
Police Academy Museum: (► 63)
South Street Seaport: (► 69)
Staten Island ferry: (► 88)
Statue of Liberty: (► 25)

Classical Music &
Performing Arts

Cut-price Broadway Tickets
The hard-to-miss 'Tkts' booth on Times Square offers same-day tickets (payment in cash only) for Broadway shows at up to half price; open Mon–Sat 3–8, Wed, Sat 10–2; Sun 11–7. Another Tkts outlet, offering similar tickets plus some for next-day matinees, operates from Bowling Green. ☎ 212/221 0013 for both.

BAM
The Brooklyn Academy of Music specialises in major new works across the musical spectrum.
✉ **30 Lafayette Avenue**
☎ **718/636 4100** 🚇 **Lafayette Avenue**

City Center
An intimate dance venue hosting a trio of innovative companies:the Alvin Ailey American Dance Theater; the Dance Theater of Harlem; and the Merce Cunningham Dance Company.
✉ **55th Street between Sixth and Seventh avenues**
☎ **212/581 3350** 🚇 **50th Street**

Eugene O'Neill Theater
Among the biggest and best of the Broadway theatres, and usually with the city's top blockbuster productions.
✉ **230 W 49th Street** ☎ **212/239 6200** 🚇 **50th Street**

Metropolitan Opera House
The opera's October opening night is a major New York occasion on the social calendar and the season continues until April. Ticket prices vary greatly, but the least costly offer a very distant perspective.
✉ **Lincoln Center** ☎ **212/362 6000** 🚇 **66th Street–Lincoln Center**

New York City Ballet
The season for this renowned company runs from November to February and from April to June, with a special performance of *The Nutcracker* held annually each Christmas.
✉ **New York State Theater, 20 Lincoln Center Plaza** ☎ **212/870 5677** 🚇 **66th Street–Lincoln Center**

New York City Opera
Next door to the Met, offering newer works, operetta and even the odd musical.
✉ **Lincoln Center** ☎ **212/870 5570** 🚇 **66th Street**

New York Philharmonic
The main season is from mid-September to May, but the highly rated Philharmonic also undertake a series of free summer recitals in each of the city's five boroughs.
✉ **Avery Fisher Hall, 10 Lincoln Center Plaza** ☎ **212/875 0538** 🚇 **66th Street–Lincoln Center**

Palace Theatre
Major Broadway theatre and home to some of New York's most extravagant extravaganzas.
✉ **1564 Broadway** ☎ **212/730 3200** 🚇 **49th Street**

Performing Garage
Long-lasting Off-off Broadway space noted for its avant-garde drama and performance art.
✉ **33 Wooster Street** ☎ **212/966 3651** 🚇 **Spring Street**

Public Theater
Six mixed-sized theatres under a single roof and home to the highly rated New York Shakespeare Festival for six weeks each summer.
✉ **425 Lafayette Street**
☎ **212/260 2400**
🚇 **Astor Place**

Sullivan Street Playhouse
Since 1960, venue for The Fantasticks, the longest-running musical in the history of American theatre.
✉ **181 Sullivan Street**
☎ **212/674 3838** 🚇 **Christopher Street**

Live Music

Baggot Inn
Enjoyable venue for lesser-known folk bands and occasional rock acts.
✉ 82 W 3rd Street ☎ 212/477 0622 🚇 W 4th Street

BB King Blues Club and Grill
Part of the new-look Times Square has been the opening of this upscale music venue that focuses on blues, but also features rock, jazz and other genres.
✉ 237 W 42nd Street ☎ 212/997 4144 🚇 42nd Street

Bitter End
Veteran of the 1960s folk scene, this small, cosy room still features up and coming folk acts interspersed with rock, jazz and comedy nights.
✉ 147 Bleecker Street ☎ 212/673 7030 🚇 W 4th Street

Blue Note
Major jazz stars frequent this atmospheric club which can be very pricy to get in to.
✉ 131 W 3rd Street ☎ 212/475 8592 🚇 W 4th Street

Bottom Line
Newcomers to major labels make the limelight here; in contrast, there are some ageing 1960s cult names.
✉ 15 W 4th Street ☎ 212/228 6300 🚇 8th Street

CBGBs
Legendary launchpad for 1970s New York punk bands, still showcasing the rising stars of the East Village and beyond.
✉ 315 Bowery ☎ 212/982 4052 🚇 Bleecker Street

Cornelia Street Cafe
The basement of this Greenwich Village restaurant makes a pleasantly intimate venue for quality jazz, poetry readings and other events.
✉ 29 Cornelia Street ☎ 212/989 9319 🚇 W 4th Street–Washington Square

Fez
Intimate and well designed venue for jazz combos and sometimes more.
✉ 380 Lafayette Street ☎ 212/533 2680 🚇 Bleecker Street

Iridium
Appealing medium-sized venue showcasing accomplished jazz names and talents on the rise.
✉ 1650 Broadway ☎ 212/582 2121 🚇 49th Street

Irving Plaza
Premier location for catching the rising international names of the indie rock and club scene.
✉ 17 Irving Plaza ☎ 212/777 6800 🚇 14th Street–Union Square

Knitting Factory
The cutting-edge sounds of jazz and funk and rock's avant-garde percolate through this musician-friendly venue.
✉ 74 Leonard Street ☎ 212/219 3006 🚇 Canal Street

Mercury Lounge
Popular showcase for the best local and rising national indie rock bands.
✉ 217 E Houston Street ☎ 212/260 4700 🚇 Second Avenue

Village Vanguard
Long-serving atmospheric jazz venue with a deserved reputation for hearing the choice talents.
✉ 178 Seventh Avenue South ☎ 212/255 4037 🚇 14th Street

On, Off and Off-Off
New York's theatre categories of Broadway, Off-Broadway and Off-off Broadway refer to the size of a theatre rather than its geographical location. Official Broadway theatres are the biggest venues and stage the biggest shows with the highest ticket prices; Off-Broadway is a step down in size and price, although many successful shows are upgraded from Off Broadway to Broadway. Off-off Broadway shows are often experimental works with small casts playing to small audiences.

Nightclubs

Cinema

Whether they want to watch new Hollywood releases, art house films or rarely screened classics, film buffs will find New York much to their liking. Choice venues for discerning film-goers are the Angelika Film Center (✉ 18 W Houston Street ☎ 212/995 2570 🚇 Broadway–Lafayette Street); Anthology Film Archives (✉ 32 Second Avenue ☎ 212/505 5181 🚇 Second Avenue) and Film Forum (✉ 209 W Houston Street ☎ 212/727 8110 🚇 Broadway–Lafayette Street).

Au Bar

Fairly bland disco music draws a predominantly designer-dressed crowd to this well-established up-market club decorated with polo sticks and croquet mallets.

✉ 58th Street ☎ 212/308 9455

Baktun

Diverse nights should hold something to please for the discerning fan of house, drum 'n bass, and other electronic-based beats presented with multimedia trimmings.

✉ 418 W 14th Street ☎ 212/206 1590 🕐 Closed Mon, Tue 🚇 14th Street/Eighth Avenue

Copacabana

A new location for a legendary 1940s supper/cabaret club in which every top singer appeared, most fun for the steamy, smartly dressed Latin disco on Tuesday and Saturday nights.

✉ 226 E 54th Street ☎ 212/239 2672 🚇 59th Street–Columbus Circle

Nell's

Comfortable, split-level dance club that draws a mixed crowd to its two attractively subdued Victorian-style main rooms that spin anything from jungle to 1980s pop.

✉ 246 W 14th Street ☎ 212/675 1567 🚇 14th Street

Roxy

Cavernous Chelsea dance club that varies by night from gay to mainstream to Latin; the dance floor becomes a roller-skating rink on some midweek nights.

✉ 515 W 18th Street ☎ 212/645 5156 🚇 23rd Street–Eighth Avenue

Sapphire

By club standards, a long-time survivor and pioneer of the nightclub invasion of the Lower East Side, with house, hip hop and rhythm and blues most nights.

✉ 249 Eldridge Street ☎ 212/777 5153 🚇 Second Avenue

SOB's

The name stands for Sounds of Brazil and that, plus similarly infectious rhythms from Africa and the Caribbean, is exactly what is delivered to an eager, stylish crowd ready to dance the night away.

✉ 204 Varick Street ☎ 212/243 4940 🚇 Houston Street

Vinyl

Some of New York's top DJs are likely to be found here, spinning house, garage and older club favourites. No bar.

✉ 6 Hubert Street ☎ 212/343 1379 🚇 Canal Street

Webster Hall

Lively and spacious venue with contrasting sounds in myriad rooms, and different themes each night.

✉ 125 E 11th Street ☎ 212/353 1600 🚇 14th Street–Union Square

Whiskey Ward

The bar carries an extensive array of bourbons and malts while the DJ room, operating Wednesday to Saturday, reveals varying nights of glam, funk, psychedelia, punk and heavy metal.

✉ 121 Essex Street ☎ 212/477 2998 🚇 Delancey Street–Essex Street

Bars

The Big Easy
A New Orleans theme bar on the Upper East Side with loud music and a generally friendly clientele around the long, curving bar.
✉ 1768 Second Avenue ☎ 212/348 0879 ⊠ 86th Street

Blind Tiger Ale House
The looks of a pre-Prohibition tavern and a strong selection of microbrewed beers.
✉ 518 Hudson Street ☎ 212/675 3848 ⊠ Christopher Street

Chumley's
The unmarked door (street number only) is a reminder of Chumley's origins as a prohibition-era speakeasy; extensive bar range and walls lined with pictures of famous ex-regulars.
✉ 86 Bedford Street ☎ 212/675 4449 ⊠ Sheridan Square–Christopher Street

d.b.a.
Popular hangout for East Village arty types with minimalist décor and a good variety of beers that will appeal to connoisseurs.
✉ 41 First Avenue ☎ 212/475 5097 ⊠ Second Avenue

Heartland
Big, brash and often rowdy, but Heartland has a tremendous stash of locally brewed beers.
✉ 35 Union Square West ☎ 212/645 3400 ⊠ 14th Street–Union Square

Hudson Bar
Expensive martinis and more are served at New York's coolest bar, amid the Philippe Starck designed furnishings of the trendy Hudson Hotel.
✉ 356 W 58th Street ☎ 212/554 6343 ⊠ 59th Street

McSorley's Old Ale House
Smoke-stained wood panels and photos of old New York all add to the atmosphere of one of the city's longest-serving bars.
✉ 15 E 7th Street ☎ 212/473 9148 ⊠ Astor Place

Peculier Pub
An enormous choice of beers and lagers from the US and beyond are served here; Fridays and weekends draws a student crowd.
✉ 145 Bleecker Street ☎ 212/353 1327 ⊠ Bleecker Street

Scruffy Duffy's
Prized for its oak floor, dart boards, pool table and friendly atmosphere, and also for its range of beers from near and far.
✉ 743 Eighth Avenue ☎ 212/245 9126 ⊠ 50th Street

Top of the Tower
With the East River on one side and Midtown Manhattan on the other, few public places have a choice of New York views as does this elegant hotel bar.
✉ Beekman Hotel, 3 Mitchell Place ☎ 212/355 7300 ⊠ 51st Street

Waterfront Ale House
Prides itself on its selection of malt whiskeys and bourbons, and also offers 50 micro-brewery ales from around the US and beyond.
✉ 540 Second Avenue ☎ 212/696 4104 ⊠ 33rd Street

White Horse Tavern
Welsh writer Dylan Thomas is supposed to have drunk his last here in this attractive Village hostelry.
✉ 567 Hudson Street ☎ 212/243 9260 ⊠ Christopher Street

The Raines Hotel Law
In an effort to reduce the level of alcohol consumed by the city's down and outs on at least one day a week, the Raines Hotel Law of 1896 made it illegal to serve liquor in New York on a Sunday, except to accompany meals in hotels. To circumvent the law, every seedy bar with a few spare rooms declared itself a hotel and offered inedible sandwiches to its inebriated customers. The law was soon repealed.

What's On When

January/February
Chinese New Year: Parades in and around Chinatown; actual date accords with the lunar cycle.
Valentine's Day Marriage Marathon: Legions of couples tie the knot on the upper levels of the Empire State Building.
Empire State Building Run-up: Indoor joggers climb the landmark building by its stairs.

March
Greek Independence Day Parade: Greek–Americans parade along Fifth Avenue between 59th and 79th streets to mark the regaining of their nation's independence in 1821.
St Patrick's Day Parade: Massive march of Irish and would-be Irish along Fifth Avenue, with countless related events.

March/April
Easter Promenade: A parade of outrageous Easter bonnets along Fifth Avenue.
Japanese Cherry Blossom Festival: Centred on Central Park's Conservatory Garden and Brooklyn's Botanic Garden.

May
Martin Luther King Day: Memorial Parade Fifth Avenue between 44th and 86th streets.
Ninth Avenue International Food Festival: Celebration of ethnic cuisines between 37th and 57th streets.
Ukrainian Festival: In the East Village, Ukrainian food and cultural events marking the anniversary of the country's adoption of Christianity.

June
Lesbian and Gay Pride Day: Enormous march along Fifth Avenue from Midtown Manhattan to Washington Square; many related events throughout Greenwich Village.
Puerto Rican Independence Day: Parade Along Fifth Avenue between 44th and 86th streets.
Shakespeare in the Park: Works of the bard staged for free in Central Park's Delacorte Theater, continues into August.

July
Independence Day: The biggest of the US's annual events celebrated with special activities throughout the city.

August
Harlem Week: Two weeks of special events marking Harlem's history and culture.

September
Feast of St Gennaro: A 10-day festival based in Little Italy's Mulberry Street; stands dispense food and an image of the saint is showered with dollar bills. Anniversary of September 11 World Trade Center attacks.

October/November
New York Marathon: Begins in Staten Island and concludes in Central Park.
Macy's Thanksgiving Day Parade: Massive balloons paraded along Central Park West and Broadway.

December
Lighting of a tree at Rockefeller Center marks the start of the Christmas season.

Practical
Matters

Above: *heavy traffic on Stillwell Avenue*
Right: *Mott Street is also signed in Chinese*

TIME DIFFERENCES

GMT 12 noon	New York 7AM	Germany 1PM	USA (LA) 4AM	Netherlands 1PM	Spain 1PM
	←	→	←	→	→

BEFORE YOU GO

WHAT YOU NEED

● Required ○ Suggested ▲ Not required	Some countries require a passport to remain valid for a minimum period (usually at least six months) beyond the date of entry – contact their consulate or embassy or your travel agent for details.	UK	Germany	USA	Netherlands	Spain
Passport/National Identity Card		●	●	▲	●	●
Visa (waiver form to be completed for non-US citizens)		▲	▲	▲	▲	▲
Onward or Return Ticket		●	●	▲	●	●
Health Inoculations		▲	▲	▲	▲	▲
Health Documentation (➤ 123, Health)		▲	▲	▲	▲	▲
Travel Insurance		●	●	▲	●	●
Driving Licence (national or International – national only for US)		●	●	●	●	●
Car Insurance Certificate		○	○	●	○	○
Car Registration Document		●	●	●	●	●

WHEN TO GO

New York

High season

Low season

4°C	5°C	8°C	16°C	21°C	27°C	29°C	28°C	25°C	19°C	12°C	4°C
JAN	FEB	MAR	APR	MAY	JUN	JUL	AUG	SEP	OCT	NOV	DEC

Very wet   Wet   Cloud   Sun   Showers/Sun

TOURIST OFFICES

In the UK
NYCVB–London
33-34 Carnaby Street,
London W1V 1PA
☎ 020 737 8300

In the USA
New York
Convention and
Visitors Bureau
810 Seventh Avenue
NY 10019
☎ 1-800 NYC VISIT

Times Square Visitor
Center
1560 Broadway
(46th Street)
☎ 212/768 1560

POLICE 911

FIRE 911

AMBULANCE 911

DENTAL EMERGENCY 1 800/439 9299

WHEN YOU ARE THERE

ARRIVING

JF Kennedy Airport, Queens:
Journey times: 'A' Train (via shuttle bus): 100 minutes approximately. Express bus to Grand Central Terminal: 60–75minutes. Taxi: 60 minutes (depending on traffic). Helicopter: 10 minutes.

JF Kennedy International Airport

Miles to city centre	Journey times
16 miles	N/A
	60–75 minutes
	60 minutes

Newark International Airport, New Jersey

Miles to city centre	Journey times
15 miles	N/A
	40 minutes
	40 minutes

MONEY

An unlimited amount of American dollars can be imported or exported, but amounts of over £10,000 must be reported to US customs, as should similar amounts of gold. US dollar travellers' cheques are accepted with photo ID in most places (not taxis), as are credit cards, (Amex, Visa, MasterCard, Diners Card). Notes (bills) commonly come in 1, 5, 10, 20, 50 and 100-dollar denominations. One dollar is 100 cents. Coins are in 1-cent (penny), 5-cent (nickel), 10-cent (dime), 25-cent (quarter), 50-cent and (rarely) 1-dollar coins.

TIME

 New York is on Eastern Standard Time, five hours behind Greenwich Mean Time (GMT-5). Daylight saving time (GMT-4) operates from early April (when clocks are advanced one hour) to late October.

CUSTOMS

 YES

Duty-free allowances for non-US residents 21 years of age or over:
spirits: 1US quart or
wine: 1US quart
cigarettes: 200
cigars: 100
or tobacco: 3 pounds or any proportionate combination.
Duty-free gifts: $100 provided the stay in the US is at least 72 hours and that gift exemption has not been claimed in the previous six months.
You may include 100 cigars within this gift exemption, but not alcoholic beverages. Articles must not be gift-wrapped as they must be available for inspection.

 NO

Meat or meat products, dairy products, fruits, seeds, drugs, lottery tickets, obscene publications, chocolate liqueurs, fireworks, switchblade knives, firearms and Pre-Columbian artefacts.

UK
☎ 212/745 9200

Germany
☎ 212/308 8700

Netherlands
☎ 212/246 1429

Spain
☎ 212/355 4080

Australia
☎ 212/351 6500

WHEN YOU ARE THERE

INFORMATION

You will find other small information centres and kiosks at the airports, Grand Central and Penn stations and the Port Authority Bus Terminal. Within the city are:

Times Square Visitor Center
● 1560 Broadway (46th Street) ☎ 212/768 1560
🕓 Daily 8–8
www.timessquarebid.org

Visitor Information Center
● 810 Seventh Avenue (between 52nd and 53rd streets) ☎ 212/484 1212
🕓 Mon–Fri 8:30–6, Sat and Sun 9–5
www.nycvisit.com

Useful Websites
Media:
The Daily News:
www.nydailynews.com
The New York Post:
www.nypost.com
The New York Times:
www.nytimes.com
The New York Observer:
www.observer.com
NY1 TV cable news channel:
www.ny1.com

City Government
www.nyc.gov

Metropolitan Transit Authority
www.mta.nyc.ny.us

General information:
www.citysearch.newyork.com
www.newyorkled.com
www.ny.com
www.zipbamboom.com

NATIONAL HOLIDAYS

J	F	M	A	M	J	J	A	S	O	N	D
2	1	1 (2)	(1)	1		1		1	1	2	1

1 Jan	New Year's Day
Jan	(third Mon) Martin Luther King Day
Feb	(third Mon) Presidents Day
17 Mar	St Patrick's Day
Mar/Apr	Easter (half day Good Friday, Easter Monday whole day)
May (last Mon)	Memorial Day
4 Jul	Independence Day
Sep (first Mon)	Labor Day
Oct (second Mon)	Columbus Day
11 Nov	Veterans' Day
late Nov	Thanksgiving (4th Thur of month)
25 Dec	Christmas Day

Boxing Day is not a public holiday in the US. Some shops open on national holidays.

OPENING HOURS

○ Shops	● Post Offices
● Offices	● Museums
● Banks	● Pharmacies

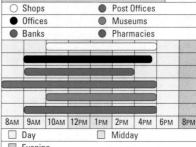

| 8AM | 9AM | 10AM | 12PM | 1PM | 2PM | 4PM | 6PM | 8PM |

☐ Day ☐ Midday
☐ Evening

Shop hours vary greatly but open till 9PM on one day; some open Sunday noon–5. Some banks open till 3:30PM. Post offices open Saturday till 1PM.

There are over 2,500 places of worship in New York of every religious denomination – see Yellow Pages.

Opening times of museums vary, check with individual museums.

There is an all-night pharmacy at Kaufman, 557 Lexington Avenue, (☎ 212/755 2266).

DRIVE ON THE RIGHT

TOILETS FREE

PUBLIC TRANSPORT

Public transit information (24hr) ☎ 718/330 1234. The $4 Fun Pass allows travel on buses (not express routes) and subways until 3AM the next morning and is available from some MetroCard vendors (inc Times Square Visitor Center) but not at subway stations.

Trains The subway offers the fastest way to travel around New York. There are five main services which mainly run parallel along Manhattan's main avenues. Buy multi-trip MetroCards or tokens ($1.50 each) at the entrance to the stations and drop one in a turnstile to access the platform. PATH and MTA trains from Grand Central Terminal serve local stations beyond the city.

Buses The bus system is simpler but slower than the subway, but has the advantage of cross-town routes. Over 36 services operate, with stops every two or three blocks, indicated by bus stops with route numbers marked. Pay with MetroCards or tokens, obtainable at subway booths, or a flat fare of $1.50. Bus maps are available from the concourse of Grand Central Terminal.

Ferries The Staten Island Ferry runs a 24-hour service ☎ 718/815 2628, and Circle Line ferries run tours from Battery Park to Ellis Island and the Statue of Liberty, with magnificent views of the Manhattan skyline from the harbour.

CAR RENTAL

There are many car rental companies and prices are competitive; it pays to shop around. The main car rental companies have toll-free (800) telephone numbers, and airports and hotel lobbies will provide details. Expect to pay for unlimited mileage but not Collision Damage Waiver or Personal Accident Insurance. Special weekend deals are widely available, but you must be over 25 to rent a car. A full valid EU driving licence is acceptable, or an International Driving Permit.

TAXIS

The New York Yellow Cabs are one of the sights of the city. When available for hire they display an illuminated sign on the roof and can then be hailed from anywhere on the street, though there are a few taxi ranks. They are legally bound to take you anywhere within the five New York Boroughs but you will be liable for bridge or tunnel tolls. Stretch limousines (with a driver) can also be booked at competitive rates if 8–10 people share.

DRIVING

Speed limit on freeways: **65mph**

Speed limit on all main roads: **65mph**

Speed limit on urban roads: **20– 25mph**, depending on the area.

Compulsory for everyone in the front seats and for children in the back.

Drivers can be pulled over at random for a breathalyser test (*alcotest*) by police. Zero tolerance is now the police code in New

Petrol (*gasoline*) is sold in American gallons. Five American gallons equal 18 litres. Most late-night and 24-hour gas (petrol) stations require you to pay the cashier before filling commences.

Driving is not recommended in Manhattan. Parking places are costly and difficult to find. If you break down with a hired car, call the rental company; or the breakdown number which should be prominently displayed on or near the dashboard.

Ruler scale

CENTIMETRES
0 1 2 3 4 5 6 7 8

INCHES
0 1 2 3

PERSONAL SAFETY

Crime levels in New York have fallen sharply over recent years. Nonetheless, it is still wise to take sensible precautions:

- Do not take the subway alone after midnight.
- Do not walk quiet streets or Central Park alone after dark.
- Carry only the cash you need, leave other cash and valuables in the hotel safe.
- Report theft or mugging to the nearest police station; this will provide a reference for your insurance company.

Police assistance:
☎ **911**
from any phone

TELEPHONES AND EMAIL

Making overseas calls from hotel phones can be expensive, doing so from public pay phones (widely found on the street and in hotel lobbies) is cheaper but will require a large amount of small change, except for the limited number of public phones that accept pre-paid phone or credit cards. Numerous cybercafes and other internet points offer email access at little cost.

International Dialling Codes	
Dial 011 followed by	
UK:	44
Ireland:	353
Australia:	61
Germany:	49
Netherlands:	31

POST

Post Offices
The main branch of the US Post Office is on Manhattan's West Side, at 421 Eighth Avenue/33rd Street. NY 10001. Open 24 hours. Other post offices can be found in Yellow Pages. Most are open 8–6 Mon–Fri, 8–1 Sat.
Mail boxes are on street corners. Hotel desks provide many mail services.

ELECTRICITY

The power supply is: 110/120 volts AC (60 cycles). Sockets take two-prong, flat-pin plugs. Visitors should bring adaptors for their 2-round-pin and 3-pin plugs. European visitors will need either dual voltage facility or a transformer.

TIPS/GRATUITIES

Yes ✓ No ✗		
It is useful to have plenty of small notes.		
Restaurants (waiters, waitresses)	✓	15%
Hotels (chambermaids, doormen etc)	✓	$1
Bar Service	✓	15%
Taxis	✓	15%
Tour guides	✓	discretion
Porters	✓	$1 per bag
Hairdressers	✓	15%

PHOTOGRAPHY

What to photograph: from the statue of Liberty to Central Park, via the Empire State Building. The New York skyline is very photogenic, especially at night.
Where you need permission to photograph: inside some public buildings and places of worship. It is wise to ask permission before photographing people
Where to buy film: all types of film and photo processing are available in drugstores, camera shops, etc.

HEALTH

Insurance
Medical insurance cover of at least $1,000,000 is strongly recommended. If involved in an accident in New York you will receive treatment by medical services and charged later.

Dental Services
Your medical insurance cover should include dental treatment, which is readily available, but expensive. One emergency dental option (more are listed in Yellow Pages) is Travelers Medical Center ☎ 212/737 1212.

Sun Advice
New York is very hot and humid in summer. It is wise to use a sunscreen and drink plenty of fluids.

Drugs
Pharmacies dispensing prescription and over-the-counter treatments are on almost every block. If you need regular medication, take your own drugs and your prescription (for US Customs). For out-of-hours emergencies Kaufman, 557 Lexington Avenue, (☎ 212/755 2266) is open 24 hours.

Safe Water
Restaurants usually provide a glass of iced water. Drinking unboiled water from taps is safe. Mineral water is cheap and readily available.

CONCESSIONS

Students/Youths Students are entitled to discounts on many attractions. You will need to show proof of student status, with an International Student Identity card, and evidence of your age.
Senior Citizens Senior citizens (seniors) will find discounts on many attractions. Men must be over 65, women over 62. You will usually be asked to show your passport.
Some restaurants also have 'senior' concessions – it pays to ask.

CLOTHING SIZES

New York	UK	Europe	
36	36	46	Suits
38	38	48	
40	40	50	
42	42	52	
44	44	54	
46	46	56	
8	7	41	Shoes
8½	7½	42	
9½	8½	43	
10½	9½	44	
11½	10½	45	
12	11	46	
14½	14½	37	Shirts
15	15	38	
15½	15½	39/40	
16	16	41	
16½	16½	42	
17	17	43	
6	8	34	Dresses
8	10	36	
10	12	38	
12	14	40	
14	16	42	
16	18	44	
6	4½	37½	Shoes
6½	5	38	
7	5½	38½	
7½	6	39	
8	6½	40	
8½	7	41	

WHEN DEPARTING

- Check airport terminal number, allow plenty of time, and arrive at least two hours before departure time.
- A yellow cab is often the quickest means of reaching the airport, or hire a stretch limousine for approximately the same price if 8–10 people share.
- US Customs are strict on entry. Ensure you have all documentation ready and are not contravening laws.

LANGUAGE

The official language of the USA is English. New Yorkers, however, are a fascinating mix of cultures from all over the world and many different languages and dialects are spoken. Taxi drivers now have to pass a test before gaining their licence and you should therefore be able to make yourself understood in either English or Spanish. Below are some words in common usage where they differ from the English spoken in the UK:

holiday	*vacation*	tap	*faucet*
fortnight	*two weeks*	luggage	*baggage*
ground floor	*first floor*	suitcase	*case or bag*
first floor	*second floor*	hotel porter	*bellhop*
second floor	*third floor*	chambermaid	*room maid*
flat	*apartment*	surname	*last name*
lift	*elevator*	cupboard	*closet*

cheque	*check*	banknote	*bill*
traveller's cheque	*traveler's check*	banknote (colloquial)	*greenback*
1 cent coin	*penny*	dollar (colloquial)	*buck*
5 cent coin	*nickel*	cashpoint	*ATM*
10 cent coin	*dime*	bill (restautant)	*check*
25 cent coin	*quarter*		

grilled	*broiled*	biscuit	*cookie*
frankfurter	*frank*	scone	*biscuit*
prawns	*shrimp*	sorbet	*sherbet*
aubergine	*eggplant*	jelly	*jello*
courgette	*zucchini*	jam	*jelly*
maize	*corn*	confectionery	*candy*
chips (potato)	*fries*	spirit	*liquor*
crisps (potato)	*chips*	soft drink	*soda*

bonnet (of car)	*hood*	main road	*highway*
boot (of car)	*trunk*	dual carriageway	*divided highway*
bumper	*fender*		
repair	*fix*	petrol	*gas, gasoline*
car park	*parking lot*	railway	*railroad, railway*
caravan	*trailer house*	tram	*streetcar*
cul-de-sac	*dead end*	underground	*subway*
lorry	*truck*	single ticket	*one-way ticket*
motorway	*freeway*	return ticket	*round-trip ticket*

shop	*store*	nappy	*diaper*
chemist (shop)	*drugstore*	policeman (colloquial)	*cop*
cinema	*movie theater*		
pavement	*sidewalk*	post	*mail*
subway	*underpass*	post code	*zip code*
gangway	*aisle*	ring up, telephone	*call*
toilet	*rest room*	long-distance call	*trunk call*
trousers	*pants*	autumn	*fall*

Acknowledgements
The Automobile Association wishes to thank the following photographers and libraries for their assistance in the preparation of this book:
THE BRIDGEMAN ART LIBRARY, LONDON 82 *Early Spring Afternoon, Central Park, 1911* (Brooklyn Museum of Art, New York); COLORSPORT 80; MAGNUM PHOTOS 50 (Eli Reed), 117a (Eli Reed); MARY EVANS PICTURE LIBRARY 10, 84b; MRI BANKERS' GUIDE TO FOREIGN CURRENCY 119; PICTURES COLOUR LIBRARY F/cover (b) Times Square; REX FEATURES LTD 11b, 14; ROBERT HARDING PICTURE LIBRARY 88b; SPECTRUM COLOUR LIBRARY 88a; UNITED STATES POSTAL SERVICE 122.
The remaining photographs are held in the Association's own library (AA PHOTO LIBRARY) and were taken by D Corrance B/cover: yellow cabs, 11a, 18, 33, 37, 39, 44, 52/3, 55a, 58, 67, 81, 83, 87, 90; R Elliott 1, 6, 8b, 13, 16, 17, 20, 21, 22, 23, 24, 29, 30, 32, 34, 40, 47, 51, 56, 59, 60, 61, 62, 64a, 65b, 68, 71; P Kenward F/cover (a) Coney Island, F/cover (d) Grand Central Station, 2, 5b, 7a, 8a, 9a, 9b, 12, 15a, 25, 27a, 27b, 35, 45, 48, 49, 54, 55b, 65a, 73, 76, 79, 84a, 86, 91b; E Rooney 5a, 9c; D Pollack 36, 46, 91a, 117b; C Sawyer F/cover (c) Statue of Liberty, 7b, 15b, 26, 42, 75.

Contributors
Copy editor: Rebecca Snelling   Page Layout: Design 23   Verifier: Sheila Hawkins
Researcher (Practical Matters): Lesley Allard   Indexer: Marie Lorimer